Y0-BEZ-059

SELF HEALING
THE SECRET OF THE
RING MUSCLES

About the Author

Paula Garbourg was born in Germany in 1907, where she studied opera singing and classical ballet. During her practice sessions she discovered that her breathing was much firmer and stronger if she stood on tiptoe. Unknown to Paula, this was her initial introduction to the "Secret of the Ring Muscles".

Paula Garbourg

SELF HEALING
The secret of the
Ring Muscles

How to control your ring muscles and free yourself from various pains and disturbances

Asthma • Migraines • Backache • Sinusitis
Arthritis • Impotence • Incontinence • and more

Peleg Publishers
Fort Lauderdale, FL

Peleg Publishers
Fort Lauderdale, FL
Hadera, Israel

Self Healing
The Secret of the Ring Muscles

by Paula Garbourg

Photos by Yael Rosen-Horn
Cover Design by Dani Caravan

Distribution:
Paula Garbourg Institute, Inc.
P.O.Box 16333
Fort Lauderdale, FL 33318, USA
P.O.Box 3186 – 38133
Hadera, Israel

Library of Congress Card No. 94–12045

Garbourg, Paula
    The Secret of the Ring Muscles
    1. Title

ISBN 0-86689-032-7

Second edition
© 1994 Paula Garbourg

PREFACE

My method developed from a basic premise about the working of the sphincter or the ring muscles in the human body. Sphincter Gymnastics came into being spontaneously. I did not intend to develop a method. The method built itself, one exercise leading to the next, which brought in its wake a third that validated its predecessor, and so on.

I am not qualified to define or describe medically the events and phenomena stemming from this muscular activity. It is the medical profession's prerogative to investigate and provide the scientific basis of this method and all its aspects.

In this book I will attempt to describe a number of things I have observed and will relate my experience in working with the Sphincter Gymnastics method.

I have quoted letters and testimonials from a few of those who have been helped by my method. Each in his/her own words gives impressions of the treatment and its results. Names of patients have been altered to preserve privacy.

The exercises at the end of the book are examples. Many should only be performed under supervision. Some require permission from the patient's physician. Older people, or those not in good health, are advised not to perform these exercises without consulting their doctors.

ACKNOWLEDGEMENTS

To Naomi Shemer and Mordechai Horowitz — my profound gratitude. Without their active help and encouragement I would almost certainly never have started, let alone finished this book.

To the doctors who accompanied me along my professional path — my appreciative thanks.

To Aya, Pat and Yoli, my students, who gave so freely of their sound common sense and time — my blessings.

To my late parents, for their constant encouragement and support, and to my dear family, for their advice and counsel and, above all, their patience — my love.

The Author

TABLE OF CONTENTS

Part II: Case Histories

Part III: Exercises

A PHYSICIAN'S COMMENT

Orthodox medicine is justifiably wary of all kinds of unconventional treatments, particularly when administered by persons who are not members of the medical profession. Only after a method has proven itself over a period of time and it is possible to ascertain that the beneficial results obtained are not merely transitory, is it appropriate for doctors, as well, to give it their consideration.

I have had the opportunity to acquaint myself with Paula Garbourg's method and work over a period of fifteen years, and the chance to assure myself of its efficacy. The basis of this method is activation of the sphincters — the muscles surrounding the various orifices of the human body. Her premise, based among other things on her highly developed powers of observation, is that all the sphincters work in unison. She applied a well known physiological principle, that the activity of one particular muscle is likely to affect the activity of another muscle, even one located some distance away. Relying on this principle, it is possible, by performing systematic exercises, to strengthen weak muscles and, for example, to correct irregularities of posture.

To bring this point home, let us take the example of a woman of about 40, suffering from the fairly common combination of low back pain, headache, sinusitis, blocked nasal passages, constipation, hemorrhoids, varicose veins, a prolapsed uterus, impaired bladder control, insomnia, irritability and depression. Her G.P. will prescribe some form of medication, or will send her to one or more of the following specialists: orthopedic surgeon, neurologist, ear, nose and throat specialist, general surgeon, gynecologist, urologist or psychiatrist. Each will suggest either medication or surgery.

It is reasonable to assume that despite protracted and diversified treatment there will be no marked improvement in this woman's condition. The numerous and various afflictions of this unfortunate woman may well stem from a slackness of the muscles of the back and the pelvic floor. Strengthening these muscles, giving up high-heeled shoes, acquiring correct habits of posture — standing, walking, etc. — all these may well cure her completely. The old Roman saying *'mens sana in corpore sano'* ('a sound mind in a sound body') will prove true in this case, as well.

Paula Garbourg's Sphincter Gymnastics has more than once succeeded where a variety of medical treatments have failed. It is often difficult to explain the beneficial results, and there is a need to study and research this method. The public would do well to make its acquaintance.

Prof. Y. Goldhammer
Neurologist

DEDICATION

This book deals with the sphincter muscles of the human body. It is based on my own first-hand experience of over fifty years of work with these muscles. Singing and classical ballet lessons gave me my initial push in this direction when I discovered that standing on tiptoe made my breathing stronger and surer. This surprising phenomenon was a bit of a puzzle to me, and I utilized it only when singing.

The second impetus was provided by bad health. As the result of an illness, I became very restricted in my movements at the age of thirty-five. One day a doctor told me I would need a wheelchair. I couldn't accept that; it was contrary to my nature. Remembering what had happened when I sang standing on tiptoe, I began practicing movements I had not performed before and with which I was unfamiliar. I started unconsciously, but the more I used these movements the more thought I gave to them. I came to the conclusion that there must be some force in the human body which restores disrupted order. I went on practicing these movements, my condition improved, and I was able to walk again.

Some years later I met Dr. Fritz Pulvermacher, a well-known orthopedic surgeon who taught me massage and anatomy. With his help I learned to understand what I had previously discovered intuitively and empirically. When I took an interest in breathing gymnastics, Dr. Pulvermacher gave me Professor Ludwig Hofbauer's book, *The Pathology of Breathing*. In this book there were things that were new to me; there were things I knew from my singing studies; and I discovered that I also knew things that were not written in the book. I talked about this with Dr. Pulvermacher, and also told him how I had helped myself several years earlier.

One day I was given the chance to demonstrate it. That day I came to the doctor for something just as he was treating a longstanding patient of his who had had a severe attack of lumbago. The doctor called me in to try my exercises with this patient. The result was positive. The patient felt much better after my treatment, got up by himself and dressed without help.

Dr. Pulvermacher became my guide and mentor. If today I am able to help others, it is thanks to him. Without him and his advice I would not have come to develop my method.

At first I treated only Dr. Pulvermacher's patients, in his treatment rooms and only in his presence. Later, with his encouragement I began to work on my own, using the Sphincter Gymnastics method I had developed.

The present book is gratefully dedicated to the memory of this great and accomplished man.

THOUGHTS ABOUT THE SYSTEM

The principles of Sphincter Gymnastics are based on Paula Garbourg's observation that in the healthy body, all the ring muscles function together as one unit. In using the term "sphincter", we do not mean ring muscle in the anatomical sense. Paula borrowed this term in order to define the sphincter as a functional unit. This system includes the eyes, the nose, the mouth and the ring muscles of the anorectal sphincters and the urogenital sphincters. In the healthy body, all the sphincters simultaneously contract and relax, activating the respiratory system, the digestive system, and the urogenital system.

The integrity of this activity is dependent upon the balance between the anterior and the posterior sphincters. Because all the sphincters function simultaneously and are interdependent in the processes of contraction and relaxation, it is possible to induce the activity of involuntary sphincters by activating the voluntary ones. It is also possible to use a healthy area to activate a malfunctioning one. For example, by contracting and relaxing the eye muscles, it is possible to obtain control over the bladder sphincter. Using these principles, Paula developed a series of exercises that induce the activation of these sphincters.

What is the mechanism that activates this harmonic system? Does it function through the central nervous system? Through the peripheral nervous system or the autonomic nervous system, or through the interrelation of both together? Does one muscle cell activate the other through a more primitive pathway? We have no clear answers to these questions; they should be subject to research.

If we observe physiological phenomena in our bodies, we

might be able to generate a research hypothesis about the operating mechanism of sphincteral gymnastics. If there is a block along any point in the cardiac conducting system, a new focus is created which paces conduction in the myocardial tissue along an alternative pathway. This might be another point within the conduction system itself that under ordinary conditions does not serve as a pacer, or it may be an additional focus of the cardiac muscle itself.

Let us look at a newborn infant. With the deep opening of its mouth at its first cry, the infant induces its first breath. By touching its lips, the sucking reflex is awakened. If its cheek is touched, the infant turns its head toward the stimulus, known as the "rooting reflex". If we hold a baby's head with our hand and suddenly withdraw the support, we induce the "Moro reflex" which consists of extension of the trunk and the arms, opening of the fists, followed by flexion of the arms and the legs. These reflexes are examples of activation of the anterior sphincters. When a baby is placed on its stomach, our hand beneath its abdomen, we induce the "Landau reflex", in which the arms, the head and the legs are extended. This is an example of activation of the posterior sphincters. Observing the motor activity of a baby, we see that it rhythmically contracts and relaxes its eyes when it sucks, extends its legs and arms, opens and closes its fists respectively, and defecates soon after eating. These kinds of activities disappear as the baby matures and are replaced by voluntary motor functions.

In summary: At birth the human nervous system functions primarily on the level of the subcortex and the spinal cord. In the process of maturation, the source of motor control is located primarily in the cortex and is primarily voluntary motor activity. As we grow, we lose the primitive reflexes. We can still view this more primitive functioning during sleep and in pathological states of damage to the central nervous system. Isn't it amazing that during the R.E.M. phase of deepest sleep characterized by dreaming, we can observe rapid eye movements? These eye movements are the basic exercise in sphincter gymnastics.

From the phenomena described, we note the parallel between sphincter gymnastics and the existence of the primitive reflexes and the involuntary activities of the body. In the Paula Method, the assumption is that through voluntary activation of the sphincters, we induce involuntary activities. This method renews and controls the subcortical functioning that was lost to us during development, and provides us with an alternative pathway to preserve the integrity of the body during disease.

The therapeutic use of this method is very extensive. It can be used to relieve muscle pain, backache and arthritis. The most important use of this method is for rehabilitation of patients with damage to the nervous system irreversible brain damage in children with cerebral palsy following C.V.A. (cerebral-vascular accidents) and spinal cord damage. In addition, this method is useful in resolving functional problems such as asthma, constipation, incontinence and prolapse of the uterus and rectum. Sphincter gymnastics is also very effective in childbirth without pain, and has additional uses.

In my experience as a pediatric pediatrician and psychiatrist, I was partner to Paula in a treatment that still moves me, though many years have elapsed since then. Paula accepted for treatment a five year-old girl diagnosed as autistic. From the history of the child, it was reported that she was a very intelligent baby. Her development up to the age of two was normal, and was even marked by signs of advanced intelligence: the child spoke fluently and could distinguish between the shape of a circle and an ellipse. After the age of two, a regression began in her development. She ceased talking, and completely changed her form of communication with those around her, including her parents. She would scream when the stimulus was not identified and her motor activity became random and unpredictable. After a series of treatments according to the Paula Method for about a month, we heard her utter the word "Mommy". She began to say "I want" and I could begin to play with her. After the end of one treatment, I hugged her and asked, "Who's sweet?" and she replied, "I am". I am not saying that this girl is completely cured and behaves like a normal child, but we do have communication with her, and she attends a regular kindergarten.

There are many cases that have been helped by Paula's method of Sphincter Gymnastics. Although Paula has forty years of experience, she is aware that her method has not been studied in any official or controlled way. She looks forward to the time when the medical community will examine this method in a clinically controlled environment and will consider it a subject for scientific research.

Dr. A. Yaroslavsky-Elias

PART I
SPHINCTERS AND
SPHINCTER GYMNASTICS

CHAPTER 1

The Sphincter and its Action in the Human Body

The Sphincter and Sphincter Gymnastics

Our life begins with the first opening and closing of the mouth — with the first cry.

Our life ends with the last breath. The mouth opens — and does not close again.

Our life is based on an unbroken chain of openings and closings:

Our eyes open and close	to see.
Our nostrils open and close	to breathe.
Our mouth opens and closes	to eat and drink.
Our muscles contract and relax	to move.
Our hands open and close	to grasp or let go, to write or play.
Our heart contracts and relaxes	to circulate the blood.

The digestive system works through the contracting and relaxing of the stomach and intestines.

Our emotions alternate: love and hate, joy and sadness.

If we look around us we see the same thing in plants and animals, and in the alternations of high and low tide, light and darkness, energy and apathy.

Nothing happens without opening and closing.

The fundamental and primary movement of opening and closing is an underlying principle of life.

My method — the method of Sphincter Gymnastics — is based on that principle.

Sphincters are ring muscles. There are many ring muscles in our body, which at one and the same time put all the other muscles and organs of the body to work. Sphincter Gymnastics is founded on this basic truth.

In Sphincter Gymnastics, one first activates the voluntary sphincter muscles: for example, those around the eyes, the mouth, the urinary duct and the anus.

Let's see what a suckling infant does. With every sucking action:

> The mouth contracts.
> The eyelids contract.
> The hands contract into fists.
> The feet contract.
> The digestive tract works.
> The anus contracts in the same rhythm as the mouth.
> The urinary tract also contracts at the same rate.
> Contracting and relaxing — the basic movement of life.

All the sphincter muscles contract and relax simultaneously. When all of them work together, we are in good health. When the sphincters do not work together, something is wrong in our body.

There are a number of diaphragms in the body. We shall deal here mainly with four zones in which diaphragmatic muscles are located. When we open and close our eyes, these diaphragms should also work simultaneously:

1. the palate diaphragm
2. the lower jaw diaphragm
3. the diaphragm separating the chest cavity from the abdomen
4. the pelvic floor diaphragm.

As stated, all these diaphragms should work in unison with the opening and closing movement of the eyes (in a person whose body is functioning properly they do function that way). The nostrils, mouth, eyebrows, scalp and the entire skin surface function together with the diaphragms. There is nothing in the human body that is not affected by the sphincters.

In the following pages we shall be calling the sphincter of the urethra the front sphincter, that of the anus the rear sphincter, and the two together the lower sphincters.

A Basic Principle: All the Sphincters Work Simultaneously and Affect One Another

The contracting and relaxing of the sphincter muscles is a natural phenomenon we cannot do without. We have to open and close our eyes. We can keep them closed for a long time, but keeping them open for long periods without blinking is not a normal condition, and may be associated with various disorders.

If we observe a sleeping child, we can see how the eyelids move in rhythm with its breathing. In exhaling, the eyelids contract slightly; and in inhaling they relax and expand slightly. This never ending chain of contractions and relaxations may be very small and weak — but it is a movement. And this weak movement takes place throughout the sleeping child's body. It is also present in adults, but is easier to observe in children. This slight movement, which goes through the entire body and all limbs and organs, is already a form of exercise.

The movement of the eyelids in sleep fills a person with vital force, like a battery being recharged. Thanks to it, a person wakes up fresh in the morning. If the eyelid movements are absent or inadequate, and certainly when they are reversed (contracting with inhalations and relaxing with exhalations), sleep is disturbed and not refreshing. There are people who do not open and close their eyes properly or adequately. They live their lives with half closed eyes, and their other sphincters also function the same way. This is not a healthy condition.

A prevalent example of disturbed functioning of the body's sphincter muscles occurs when one has a common cold. The movement of the front sphincter affects not only the bladder but, among other things, the nose as well. When a person catches cold and does not feel well, his posture is also bad. He more or less caves in, which hinders the sphincters' unified operation. There is no longer real contact between the four diaphragms. The roof of the palate and the diaphragm of the lower jaw are not properly linked with the diaphragm and the pelvic floor. This leads to increased lordoses (inward curvatures of the spine) and to irregular blood circulation.

Sore throats are sometimes caused by pressure at the lordosis of the neck because the neck muscles are not functioning properly. Proper contracting and relaxing of the front sphincter improves the condition of the lordosis and restores the normal functioning of the diaphragms. Proper opening and closing of the urethral sphincter automatically results in proper opening and closing of the nostrils.

Until now we have spoken only of relatively healthy people who have no trouble contracting and relaxing the front sphincter. There are, however, many people whose front ring muscles have been so weakened that they can no longer be controlled at will. In such cases other sphincters can be used to help restore the weakened muscles to normal functioning. This is based on the principle that the sphincters work simultaneously, and can therefore prod each other into action. A sphincter that can no longer be controlled voluntarily may be activated through another sphincter that still responds to control. For instance, a weakened front sphincter may be activated by working the sphincter muscles that govern the eyelids, over which most people can still exercise some control. In this case, opening and closing the eyes serves to contract and relax the sphincters over which control has been lost.

Breathing

As stated, all the diaphragms work together with the sphincters. If, for example, the eyelids are contracted — the diaphragms contract as well:
The palatal diaphragm contracts,
The lower jaw diaphragm contracts.
The diaphragm between the chest and the abdomen contracts.
The pelvic floor diaphragm contracts.
The mouth and lips contract.
The abdominal muscles contract.
The front and rear sphincters contract.

The mouth cavity is of optimum size, permitting the best possible resonance when speaking and singing. The diaphragms in the palate and the lower jaw affect production of head and chest tomes. Contracting the abdominal muscles and the lower sphincters provides us with the firmest foundation for breathing.

If the sphincters and diaphragms do not contract and relax sufficiently, the singing tone becomes flat and impure. If the sphincters and diaphragms work together properly, the result is perfect tone and easy, effortless voice production in both speaking and singing. These results are of course not immediate. Long practice is sometimes required to obtain them.

If the working of the sphincters and diaphragms is impeded, speech difficulties may often follow. The voice gets hoarse and weak, sometimes disappearing altogether.

When breathing as though savoring the scent of a flower, the nostrils dilate, the shoulders expand and draw back, and the rib muscles (which contract and expand the chest) also expand.

If, however, air is forced upwards through the nose, the nose clogs up, the shoulders rise, and the nostrils remain almost motionless, and may, in fact, contract slightly.

The act of breathing is not confined to the diaphragms and nostrils. In breathing, not only do all the sphincter muscles function, but all the other muscles, as well. The entire body participates from head to toe. During deep breathing it is actually possible to see the arms rotate slightly inward and the backs of the hands turn forward when inhaling, and the arms rotate slightly outwards and the palms turn forward, when exhaling.

When the back of the hand is turned forward, i.e., when inhaling, the front sphincter begins to contract, and there is a tendency for the two big toes to move towards each other. The reverse happens when exhaling — the palms rotate slightly towards the front, the rear sphincter contracts and there is a tendency for the heels of the feet to move towards each other. When inhaling, the movement of the big toes towards each other shifts the body weight to the back of the feet while the weight shifts forward when exhaling.

If an unpracticed person tries this while standing, he/she may find it hard to sense the process — both because the changes are extremely slight and because the entire weight of the body is pressing down on the soles of the feet. Sometimes, however,

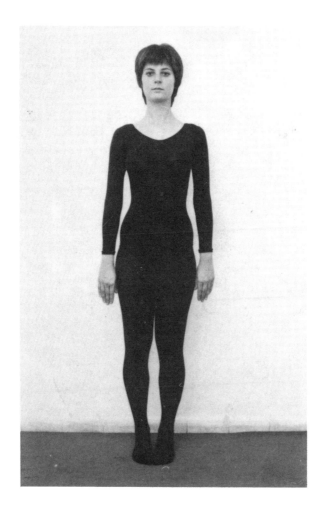

Inhaling: arms rotated somewhat inward,
backs of hands turned forward

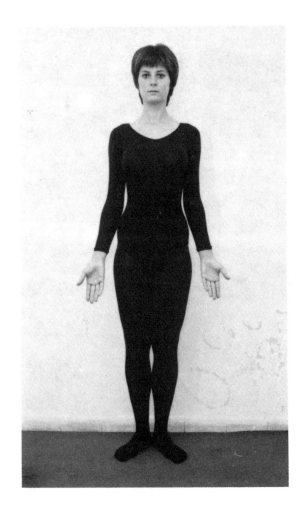

Exhaling: arms rotated somewhat outward,
palms of hands turned forward.

even unpracticed people may, if they are attentive, feel a slight pressure in the soles of their feet as described above.

When a person with some practice lies on his/her back with feet planted parallel (see illustration p. 138), it may be clearly seen how the muscles — both interior and exterior — of the calves and thighs move slightly with the rhythm of normal breathing. It is the muscles on the inside of the legs (the adductors) that bring the feet together and the outside muscles (the abductors) that move them apart.

Taking a deep breath makes the eyes open slightly more than normal, and a very long exhalation makes them contract slightly more.

The same movement appears in the ears, provided the sphincter muscles are really functioning properly.

There is also a constant slight movement of the legs, during normal deep breathing; they move in and out, up and down, as described above.

Breathing affects the entire body — and the position of the feet as well.

Putting the heels together makes it easier to exhale. Putting the toes together makes it easier to inhale.

Any one suffering from breathing problems should not experiment with this!

There is a whole series of exercises than can be used to bring together the heels or toes (as the need may be), and thereby affect breathing. This will be discussed later.

It should be borne in mind that a person who is unpracticed or not in good health will not notice immediate results.

In singing and speaking the abdomen contracts in an upward movement starting from the front sphincter.

If the voice exerts pressure in the opposite direction, i.e., downward, the sound produced may still be full and round, but the speaker or singer will sooner or later begin to experience discomfort or pain, especially in the knees. This pain is often related to bladder problems. Physical and behavioral stability also suffer, and impatience and nervousness appear. When breathing is irregular everything is irregular, for proper breathing is the cornerstone of health.

When a healthy person emits an occasional cough, it can be taken as the body helping itself. During a cough the front sphincter closes forcibly, the respiratory and abdominal muscles are pressed into sudden action, and the upward pressure expels the phlegm.

Sneezing, like coughing, results from inadequate activity of the front sphincter and is designed to stimulate its action. This, too, is the body coming to its own aid.

If the respiratory muscles are not functioning properly, coughing exerts pressure in the opposite direction — from the top down. The front and rear sphincter lose their muscle tone. Their closure is incomplete, they become slack, and control of bladder and bowel movements may become faulty.

CHAPTER 2

Everyday Habits

Smoking

Smoking is bad for us, and can easily be stopped — if we want to.

When an attempt is made to break the habit an increased demand for food is experienced. Weight increases. Why?

A smoker's oral sphincter is usually slack. To obtain the necessary muscle tone, the smoker puts a cigarette into his/her mouth — and the lips close and contract. This contraction of the lips increases the smoker's ability to concentrate. He/she is able to think more clearly and work better because the oral sphincter is making all the other sphincters wake up and work.

The increased ability to concentrate and work gained by smoking can be achieved in a healthier way. A toothpick two to four millimeters long is placed between the lips. The lips instinctively play with the toothpick. This makes them contract much as they do in smoking. It does not interfere with speech. The toothpick can be shifted onto the tongue (it is practically weightless), or left between the upper lips and upper teeth.

Any cigarette-holder-type mouthpiece can be effective. It will keep the lips busy, will encourage them to contract, thereby making the body's other sphincter muscles also contract. The mouthpiece should be held with the lips and not with the teeth.

The irresistible desire to put a cigarette between the lips shows that the lower sphincters have become flabby.

There are numerous exercises designed to bring back the

sphincter muscles' ability to function. When the lower sphincters are contracted the mouth also contracts, and the need to put a cigarette between the lips disappears.

The use of nicotine and other drugs may also result from poor functioning of the lower sphincters. When these sphincters are not working properly, it causes a feeling of emptiness and perpetual dissatisfaction. This feeling accompanies a person into all areas of life — working, sex, eating, posture and behavior.

Overeating

Overeating belongs in this category, as well. Just one improperly working sphincter muscle is enough to throw all the others off balance. As a result, the muscles do not function properly, i.e., they do not contract and relax adequately. In such conditions the sphincter muscles begin to act like a pump, pumping food into the body without control or limit.

Here, too, the principle that an upset balance should be corrected, applies. By exercising the muscles of the lower sphincters it is possible to overcome overeating.

When chewing is done correctly — with lips closed but the mouth cavity as widely opened as possible — the lower sphincters and the intestines can be felt working in rhythm with one another, causing the abdomen to contract.

To practice proper chewing, the oral cavity should first be opened as widely as possible with all one's might, behind closed lips, so as to get a sense of the reaction in the direction of the lower sphincters. Sometimes it is too difficult to open the oral cavity when the lips are closed. In such cases, opening the mouth cavity as widely as possible with parted lips must be learned first, and doing so with closed lips only afterwards. When the muscles get used to this tiring exercise, it is no longer necessary to expand the inside of the mouth too much. Exercise turns into habit, and correct chewing becomes second nature. But it is essential to keep in touch with the body's reactions. Once the sphincters are felt to be cooperating, an attempt may be made to precede each chewing motion with a tensing of the front sphincter. After much long practice it is possible to make chewing motions happen by contracting this sphincter. The mouth opens quite widely behind closed lips, while externally, only natural chewing motions are visible.

The abdomen and shoulders of people who chew only superficially — whose oral cavities do not open widely enough on the inside — fall forward and the entire body droops.

One often sees people eating with their arms leaning on the table as if they wanted to keep from 'falling into their plates'. This is not a mark of bad manners. People who do this are just not used to making large chewing motions with closed lips because they are tired or nervous, they do not devote enough time to eating, or the table and chairs are too high or too low.

Smokers are often heard to say that they need a smoke to feel good after a meal. This means that the body is demanding that the oral sphincter be contracted to make it possible for the digestive system to operate. Here, too, a toothpick between the lips will help.

By opening the mouth as widely as possible behind closed lips, one can feel the lower sphincters participating. when they contract properly, the sphincters of the stomach, gullet and larynx contract automatically, and there is no further demand for more food. The sphincters are back to normal operation.

It is thus possible to eat enough without fear of getting fat. It only takes opening the mouth cavity widely enough at each chew to bring all the sphincter muscles into action, thereby enabling the body to burn up calories.

If the mouth cavity is not opened widely enough when chewing, and the other sphincters are not made to share in the act of chewing, the abdomen grows larger even if less is eaten.

It is also important to chew in a balanced manner on both sides of the mouth. If the mouth is opened properly, chewing on both sides happens automatically. One-sided chewing may sometimes cause spinal curvature.

If the mouth cavity is opened widely enough, there is no need to chew food a great deal before swallowing it.

Drinking

When drinking, the liquid should not be poured into the mouth, but drunk in small sips with a strong contraction of the lower lip. When swallowing, the lower lip relaxes. The upper lip usually duplicates the lower lip's contractions and relaxations. The front and rear sphincters can soon be felt to be contracting together with the whole body.

Waking up in the morning, drinking a glass of water in small sips as described above is a morning exercise in itself. In this exercise the oral sphincter serves as the point of departure, from which all the other sphincters begin to work together.

The sphincter muscles can be activated even before drinking water, while brushing the teeth. If correctly done, rinsing the mouth and gargling will activate the sphincters of the mouth and throat, and with them the lower sphincters, as well — i.e., the entire body.

Standing and Sitting

Most etiquette is based on healthy habits. A polite person sits with his/her feet together. It is good manners. In recent years illustrated journals and magazines have been showing models sitting or standing with legs and feet exaggeratedly spread open. That's the latest fashion. These young women are often no longer capable of standing straight, because of wearing heels that are too high. Many suffer from prolapsed abdominal organs. When seated they cave in, their backs become hunched, and this makes them sit open-legged. This is a case of physical distress setting the styles. The high heels make them stand almost on point, a stance that makes the rear sphincter contract strongly. Nobody can stand on tiptoe all the time without damage to the proper working of the sphincters. So the muscles that pull the legs together (the adductors) are no longer working properly, which is what causes the wide straddle.

There are people, young and old, who wear low-heeled shoes — and still stand or sit with their legs spread too wide. One cause may be driving, as it is impossible to keep the knees together while sitting behind a steering wheel. Insufficient sleep, or work that requires standing for long periods of time, may cause fatigue — which also leads to sitting or standing with legs too far apart. The muscles get too tired to function properly.

A few words about various sitting positions:

The early Egyptians and Chinese used to sit, as seen in ancient pictures, on straight wooden chairs, with legs together and pelvis at right angles to them. It is easy to get up from this position. The legs remain close together when standing and walking, as well.

The Japanese sit on their legs. The feet are together and the buttocks rest on the heels. From this position it is possible to rise effortlessly at any time.

In the sitting position of the ancient Egyptians, the Chinese and the Japanese, the muscles that pull the legs together (the adductors) work very forcefully. This results in restrained, disciplined and quiet behavior.

Other Oriental peoples sit cross-legged on carpets or cushions, their knees spread very widely. In this Oriental sitting position, the adductors cannot work normally and equilibrium is upset. When the adductors aren't working as they should be, the abdomen often falls forward. It is not hard to get up from this position, because the rear sphincter is working. But this position promotes less restrained, less disciplined behavior.

Walking and Running

The sphincters are also used in walking.

The correct walking motion is as follows: the foot is brought forward by raising the knee slightly, the heel is placed on the ground, and then the foot is rolled to the tips of the toes. A slight backward push with the tips of the toes makes the knee lift. This process is repeated over and over again in walking.

These alternating movements occur in such a way that when the heel of one foot touches downward, the other foot rolls forward. This involves the sphincters contracting and relaxing. In stepping on the heel, the front sphincter contracts; in pushing

with the tips of the toes, the rear sphincter contracts. When the knee is lifted, the front sphincter contracts; when the foot rolls to the tips of the toes, the rear sphincter contracts.

By watching eye movements it is possible to see how all the sphincter participate in the act of walking. The eyes open and close in rhythm with the feet. It is a perfect harmony, of which only well practiced individuals are aware.

In climbing uphill the rear sphincter works harder than the front sphincter, pushing the body forward. Descending, it is the front sphincter that works harder, keeping the person from involuntarily running and falling downhill.

One sometimes sees people — and not just old people — who can climb up stairs after an illness or surgery but have trouble and even suffer pain going down stairs. Contracting the front sphincter, which is necessary in descending, is almost always harder than contracting the rear sphincter. Sphincter Gymnastics offers such people the possibility of going up and down stairs without pain.

In running medium and long distances the whole foot is involved, starting from the heel and rolling all the way to the toes. This generates alternating contractions and relaxations of the front and rear sphincters. In contrast, sprinting involves a very strong forward push by rear sphincter contraction, in that the heels do not come into contact with the ground.

To turn jogging into a healthy sport, the whole foot must be brought into play, starting from the heel and rolling the foot forward to the tips of the toes. If the heels don't touch the ground, lumbar lordosis is reinforced and disagreeable side effects may result.

Not rolling the entire foot from the heel prevents all the muscles of the body from participating.

In walking correctly with all the muscles participating, the body stretches, breathing becomes deeper, the shoulders pull back, the chest relaxes and the abdomen pulls in.

Treading on a foot all at once without rolling it causes the opposite to happen. The shoulders fall forward, the chest narrows, the body slumps, the abdomen sags, breathing is shallow, and the weight of the body shifts from side to side. The lower sphincters, which work normally when walking correctly, are unable to function as they should.

All the above would be incomplete without mentioning the problem of shoe heels. Even low heels play a part in changing the body — not to speak of the grave damage caused by high heels. We are born without elevated heels and that is our natural state. When we alter it, we also alter the position of limbs and organs and jeopardize their proper functioning.

As to children, flexible soled shoes without added heels are available on the market only for the first two sizes. From size 3, all children's shoes have heels, and the soles are sometimes stiff. For some years it has been possible to find shoes on the market with relatively high-heels even for girls of nursery school age!

Stiff soles and raised heels interfere with the rolling motion of the foot when walking. Pediatricians recommend walking barefoot for normal development of the child's body.

Standing with high heels —
unnatural position of the internal organs.

uterus

bladder

urethra

vagina

rectum

Standing naturally without heels —
all internal organs in the correct place.

Singing and Dancing

What is the connection between singing and dancing and the sphincter muscles? The answer is: without correct use of the sphincters, particularly the lower sphincters, balanced performance in song and dance is inconceivable.

Dancing
The technique of classical ballet is essentially built on balance

between the front and rear sphincters. This is true of all types of dancing, from folk dancing and artistic dance to the dances of the Far East through to ballet. If the rear sphincter is dominant, it pushes the body forward and upward, but posture is less than perfect. An overly strong lordosis is produced at the small of the back and the neck, making the buttocks protrude and giving the impression that the dancer is almost sitting. A good dancer should appear to be able to soar through the air. This impression can only be conveyed when the front sphincter is working as hard as the rear sphincter. The back and neck lordoses are then normal and an impression of perfect balance is conveyed.

Dance steps are not executed exclusively on the heels or exclusively on point. There is a constant shifting between the heel (front sphincter) and the tips of the toes (rear sphincter). These two sphincters cause all the other sphincters and organs to operate in high gear, which stimulates and sharpens overall activity: breathing, vision, hearing, emotion, sex and voice.

Singing
Singing cannot be based on only part of the sphincters either. Without adequate front-sphincter activity a metallic, sometimes discordant tone results.

To produce perfect tone, perfect balance between the front and rear sphincters is needed. Greater use of the rear sphincter again leads to an increased lumbar lordosis, resulting in the full figure that characterized the opera stars of old.

The lordosis at the small of the back causes a lordosis of the neck, making it impossible to produce a free, full, clean tone.

By increasing rear sphincter action, aggressive and dramatic expression is obtained, with no soft and lyrical overtone.

The singer requires perfect balance between the front and rear sphincters in order to achieve full and natural expression.

It is the singer's task to train their voices which are their instruments, so as to be able to put all their physical and mental powers into performing works of music.

CHAPTER 3

Parts of the Body

The Face

When all internal organs are functioning properly, it shows on the face. Deviation in the features indicates deviation from the norm in the internal organs. In many cases, such deviations may be corrected by appropriate sphincter exercises, orthodontic treatment, or a combination of the two. The facial features, also being composed of muscles, may be restored to health by Sphincter Gymnastics.

The Lips
The shape of the lips has a decisive effect on the whole body.

The normal face, as we know it from classic Greek and Roman sculpture, is characterized by curved lips of clearcut symmetric outline, without any drooping or slackness. The upper lip arches upwards, the lower lip arches downwards, and there is a slight hollow under the lower lip. This hollow is an indication of the normal state of the hollows at the neck and the waist.

More often than not, the opposite is to be seen. There is almost no hollow under the lower lip; and there are pronounced lordoses of the neck and waist. Another result of this condition is a rounded back, which makes for a narrowed chest, a sagging abdomen, and faulty positioning of the legs. A well curved upper lip usually goes with shoulders that are pulled back as they should be. There are no pronounced lordoses of the neck and waist, the chest is free, the pelvis and legs have a normal stability. This assures proper coordination, and enhances concentration, optimism and serenity.

A black person is a good example, with upper lip curling strongly up, and back especially straight. The curled upper lip is a mark of shoulder blades that are drawn back and pulled down in the good posture which is characteristic of many blacks. Up until now we have been talking about a well arched upper lip. A flat upper lip, on the other hand, indicates disturbed balance in the body. It does not necessarily mean a serious defect, but it is recommended that the condition be corrected by suitable exercise.

When a child of nursery-school age loses several front teeth, the lips may often contract. This makes the rear sphincter contract. The child is liable to drift into constant spasmodic motion and as a result be restless and hyperactive. If such a child starts school before his/her second teeth have grown in, he/she may be subject to inner disquiet and have trouble sitting still and following the classwork. A temporary dental prosthesis is a good solution for this condition, with Sphincter Gymnastics as a follow-up. The exercises are easy ones that children enjoy doing and that enable them to help themselves in a short time.

The Nose

The nose is one of the instruments of breathing and it, too, may be a point of departure for all around sphincter activation. The nostrils move while breathing. Together with the nostrils and in the same rhythm, the ribs also move, and with them all the internal and external body organs.

One sometimes sees noses with nostrils that are too flared. This affects the whole body. This is also true in the opposite case. When the nostrils stay almost closed and do not open, this too is reflected throughout the body.

36

Sometimes the nose is too broad or too fleshy. Sometimes the tip of the nose has a round shape. All these show that the front and rear sphincters are not working adequately.

We may also see a fleshy layer on the nose. When the front and rear sphincters are working properly, the nostrils also work properly and this layer disappears.

Many deviations from the norm may be restored to normal when there is enough patience to exercise. A pug nose often entails an open mouth; the oral and lower sphincters are not working adequately, so the lordoses get deeper.

Nose surgery sometimes brings on headaches or back-aches. When the muscles of the nose aren't working well enough — even temporarily — the lordoses get deeper, which may be the reason for these pains.

When the nose muscles are functioning properly, they pull the shoulders back, make the lordoses smaller, and strengthen the connection between the back and pelvic muscles. The sphincters, and with them all the organs and muscles, then operate normally.

Long noses often go with narrow, insufficiently curled upper lips. The cheek muscles are not well developed. This usually goes with poor posture and is a mark of inadequate sphincter activity. As the nose muscles are not working properly, the lower sphincters aren't operating well, either.

But in most cases the opposite is true: the lower sphincters are not working properly and that is why the nose changes.

The Jaws, Teeth and Tongue

The position of the teeth in the jaw directly affects the tongue. The tongue in turn acts as a rudder for the spine and the whole body. When the tongue is pushed to one side, even very slightly, it immediately affects the spine — also pushing it to the side.

In some people the midlines of the upper and lower incisors do not meet precisely. When a right-handed person pushes the tip of his/her tongue behind the upper-left wisdom tooth,the midlines of the upper and lower incisors may usually be seen to meet. This has a straightening effect on the spine, provided scoliosis (curvature) is not too pronounced.

A 'night guard', a dental appliance that keeps the upper and lower teeth from touching during sleep, can produce a result similar to that of the exercise. It aligns the lower incisors with the upper incisors without any special exercise.

When the tip of the tongue is pressed against the left side of the upper jaw, the shoulders are pulled to the left, the hips are pushed to the right and the head turns to the right. If the tongue is pressed against the right side of the upper jaw, the shoulders are pulled to the right, the hips are pushed to the left, and the head turns to the left.

When the tip of the tongue is pressed up against the soft palate, the head tilts back, the shoulders are pulled back and squeezed together. At first, the lordosis at the waist gets a little stronger and the heels come together. Soon after the abdomen is pulled in and the two big toes brought together until they are finally parallel with the heels — which means that the abdominal and back muscles are working simultaneously.

If a tooth protrudes somewhat, the tip of the tongue pushes into that spot. This makes the body twist, and may lead to a spinal curvature that can only be corrected by an orthodontist. In many cases of scoliosis, it is the orthodontist who may possess the key to proper treatment.

Through my collaboration with the late orthodontic surgeon, Dr. Aga Spitz, I became acquainted with many cases that proved the connection between the state of the teeth and that of the spine. One interesting case was the following: a man who had suffered from backaches for many years exercised with me for a few weeks. The pains disappeared during the treatment — but only for a short time. Two weeks later he came back complaining of the same pain. This time I referred him to Dr. Spitz. She filed one tooth — and his backaches permanently went away.

Naturally, not every backache can be disposed of by filing a tooth. Orthodontic treatment of scoliosis usually takes longer. But when undesirable symptoms arise from a dental problem, no kind of gymnastics treatment will do any good without the assistance of an orthodontist. Of course, this does not apply to every type of scoliosis, but it may be worthwhile to ask an orthodontist to determine if the scoliosis stems from the condition of the teeth.

The state of the jaw has a critical effect, not only on posture and general health, but often on the state of mind, as well. It is appropriate to mention caps, bridges and false teeth in this context.

One can see the sudden change in elderly people when they start wearing false teeth. The mouth becomes wide and taut, the cheeks fall, and a double chin and tense look are produced. The nose becomes flatter, longer and wider.

The reason is that dentures are usually wider and thicker than the natural teeth were, which affects the equilibrium of the sphincters. The upper lip can also be seen to stretch, instead of curling as it should, after caps have been fitted in the upper jaw. When the mouth cannot contract naturally and spontaneously by itself, the other sphincters in the body can't do so either. Since all the sphincters are interconnected, it is evident that the connection between the lower sphincters and what happens in the mouth and jaw can also work the other way round. That is, conditions in which internal organs of the body sag or drop may often cause jaw defects. This may be explained by the fact that properly functioning lower sphincters generate a sort of gentle and constant massage in the region of the mouth. When the lower sphincters contract, the oral sphincter contracts simultaneously. When the functioning of the lower sphincters is hampered, the mouth and jaws are immediately affected.

The reason for grinding of teeth may often be found in a too-pronounced cervical lordosis caused by overtiredness, over exertion and insufficient contraction of the sphincters. This, too, can easily be stopped by means of Sphincter Gymnastics.

The position of the jaws also affects the eyes, and vice versa. When the eyes are moved from side to side, the lower jaw makes a slight corresponding movement.

The various positions of the jaws and the physical postures affected by them have results that may manifest themselves in a person's behavior.

In the normal position of the jaws, the lower front teeth are covered by the upper teeth, but do not touch them. There are three kinds of deviations from this norm:

1. The prognathous bite, in which the lower jaw projects beyond the upper jaw.
2. The tête-à-tête bite, in which the biting surfaces of the upper and lower jaws are flush.
3. The retrognathous bite, in which the lower jaw recedes farther than normal.

Each of these deviations from the normal position of the jaws has its own characteristic postural defects, with a corresponding emotional effect.

In a prognathous bite, the jutting lower jaw causes not only slumped shoulders, a rounded back and increased lordosis of the neck and the small of the back (the lumbar region), but bow legs and flat feet as well.

In a tête-à-tête bite, the shoulders are pulled slightly back, abdomen thrust forward, chest barreled, lordoses increased, heels together, knees pressed inwards, head raised and tilted tensely back and up in a way that gives the impression of rigidity and aloofness. This type of person's stature appears taller than it really is, and he/she always stands out in a group.

Johann Sabastian Bach had this kind of bite. In her book, *The Small Diary of Anna Magdalena Bach,* his second wife tells of the impression he made on her at first sight:

"He looked especially tall to me, though he was actually of average height: somehow he looked tall, broad and forceful. He left a rock-like impression, and when standing with others his stature always seemed to stand out."

We read further: "...he looked very decisive, apparently because of his strong, jutting chin — his teeth met exactly jaw-to-jaw, not like most people whose lower jaw recedes into the upper. So his face looked utterly different from most people's faces. The power of his features aroused some hesitation in the hearts of anyone who wished to approach him..."

In a retrognathous bite the upper jaw projects and the lower jaw recedes exaggeratedly under it. With jaws in this position, the lordoses of the neck and the small of the back are deeper, the head tiled forward, mouth open, nostrils dilated, bridge of nose narrow, fingers and toes straight, body standing almost on tiptoe (sprinters often have this kind of bite and posture).

Well practiced people with a normal bite may find out for themselves, if they care to experiment, how deviations from the normal position of the jaws affect posture and state of mind. By advancing the lower jaw beyond the upper, a prognathous bite can be produced temporarily. Within a short time they will find their bodies developing a posture resembling the one described for that kind of bite. The same will be true if the lower jaw is pulled back to a position producing a retrognathous bite.

When the lower jaw is moved forward, body posture begins to change quite rapidly. First, the shoulders move forward, the back becomes rounded, and as a result the chest sinks. The abdomen pulls in at first, but that passes quickly and it falls forward, as do the arms. The knees spread, the heels come together, the lordoses get stronger, and strong pressure is exerted on the ears and the entire head. The eyebrows contract, the weight of the body rests on the front of the foot. The body is in position to attack.

The Eyes

It goes without saying that proper treatment of eye problems demands specialized knowledge. Yet there is a connection between the eyes and the lower sphincters. A wink between a couple, for instance, affects the sphincter of the sexual organs; hence the erotic significance of the wink in folklore. It is therefore worth checking whether the reason for certain eye problems may not lie in faulty functioning of the lower sphincters.

Contact lenses do not have a good effect on the body. Like false teeth, they make the sphincter muscles around them stretch somewhat. This minimal stretching of the sphincter muscles around the eyes hampers their proper functioning and affects the lower sphincters.

People who wear spectacles also suffer from a negative side effect. When spectacles are worn continuously for long periods of time without being removed, tension is produced in the eye zone. Swelling occurs in the eyelids. They begin to close, making the eyes look out through slits. The tension and the incomplete eye closure are liable to make the lordoses of the neck and the small of the back grow, the upper pelvis tilts forward, and all the sphincter muscles of the body work incorrectly — neither opening nor closing properly.

Inadequate activity of the lower sphincters may make the eyes protrude. The posture is slack, head and shoulders slanted forward, the knees slightly bent in standing and walking. People with protruding eyes always look tired and have a tendency to be shortwinded and hoarse. When the eyelids are not contracting adequately, the diaphragms cannot do so either.

Small eyes as well as dry eyes (a feeling of 'sand in the eyes') are signs of an inadequately functioning front sphincter.

The Ears

The various sphincters affect one another. In cases of earache, a discharge sometimes appears in the eye on the same side. This discharge often goes away together with the earache when sphincter exercises are performed.

Sleeping with ear plugs to block out noise hampers the activity of the ear (i.e. the contraction and relaxation of the muscles around the plug). During such sleep the mouth is usually open, and the head feels fuzzy upon awakening. There is no feeling of being refreshed, since the eyelids have not been able to contract and relax adequately either.

The Skin

Sphincter exercises affect the skin a great deal.

By means of eyelid exercises, for example, scars left by tuberculosis vaccinations can be blurred — even when they are very prominent and many years old. The same applies to smallpox vaccinations, with both children and adults.

Skin transplants performed because of wounds or other reasons may leave ugly scars. These can be affected almost entirely by sphincter exercises, even after many years.

The exercises also have a beneficial effect on various skin diseases such as acne or eczema. It is quite common for someone to come to exercise because of specific pains, and in the course of normalizing sphincter activity to have skin problems disappear as well.

Restoring part of the body to normal working order by means of Sphincter Gymnastics usually contributes to normalizing the whole body. The reason for this may be that the sphincters bring blood circulation back to normal, and this is likely to have a beneficial effect on the skin.

Certain facial wrinkles often show something is wrong in the body. Along with the general improvement resulting from Sphincter Gymnastics, the wrinkles diminish as well. This improvement stems from better operation of the lower sphincters.

Fingers and Hands

The condition of the hands also reflects the condition of the body.

For example, if the index finger of the right hand is a bit crooked, it suggests a curvature of the spine. In such a case, it

45

may be straightened gently with the left thumb and forefinger (see figure). When the finger is straightened, the spine will straighten, too. Any finger that deviates from its normal position affects the spine, and vice versa, the spine affects the position of the fingers. The same applies to fingers that bend outwards: Sphincter Gymnastics has a beneficial effect on this condition.

With certain finger exercises it is possible to affect the sense of balance beneficially, as well as mental capacity.

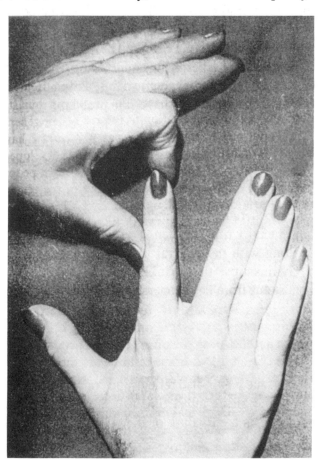

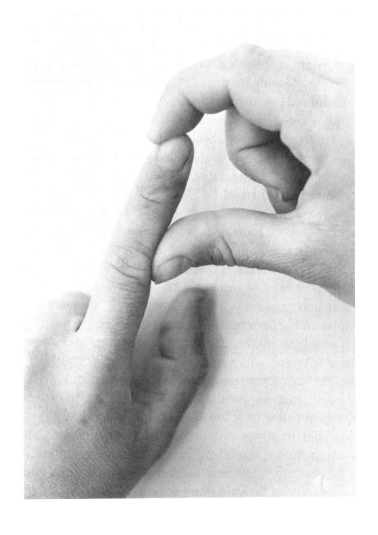

CHAPTER 4

Pregnancy, Childbirth and Nursing

Among primitive peoples, normal childbirth occurs without external help. Relying on the experience passed from generation to generation, the women leave it to their own bodies to do this natural job without interference.

In civilized countries, healthy women can also give birth to their children without fear, and almost without pain, provided the sphincter muscles of the entire body are functioning properly, and the childbirth is natural.

The women should prepare themselves for childbirth with sphincter exercises, starting as early as possible. These exercises put the sphincters into normal, healthy shape, provided, of course, that there is no infection or genetic disturbance. Breathing must also be normal. When sphincter action is normal, breathing is regular and posture is erect. The spine is supported by the abdominal and back muscles, and the lordoses are normal. This keeps the edges of the upper pelvis and the abdomen from dropping forward and varicose veins from forming. It also prevents the backaches that often appear in pregnancy.

It sometimes happens after childbirth that the mother's milk either does not flow or is insufficient. If this condition is not due to illness but to stress, exhaustion or something of that sort, gently contracting and relaxing the eyelids may be helpful. While doing this exercise, the new mother quite soon feels the milk being released and flowing into her breasts. She herself, and the infant, are soothed together.

The use of tampons during menstruation hampers the

activity of the vaginal sphincter muscles. Women have a feeling of being unable to breathe, hear or see as usual, and may even faint. This is because one malfunctioning sphincter keeps other sphincters from functioning properly.

The elementary influence of the sphincters is apparent not only in humans but in animals as well. For animals, proper functioning of the sphincters can be a matter of life and death. Mother mice, cats and dogs must stimulate their newborn by licking their lower sphincters. Without this, the pup (kitten, etc.) will not be able to empty its bowels or pass urine. That is, it will be unable to live.

When the mother is absent, it is customary to massage the front and rear sphincters of pedigreed pups with a piece of damp cloth as a substitute for the mother's licking. This stimulates all the sphincter muscles and sets all the pup's systems and organs into motion.

Without all the sphincter muscles working correctly, animals cannot live. This is true for all mammals, and of course for human beings as well.

Pregnancy and Childbirth (by Dr. H. Tifereth)

Paula Garbourg's sphincter muscle exercises lead to harmonic function of the human body if done properly and continuously. When Paula advised me to try her exercises during delivery, I couldn't resist it, because I was sure that if it didn't help, it would do no harm to the woman in labor. So ladies were randomly chosen to practice Paula's exercises during their active labor. Within 6 months, about 30 patients delivered doing these exercises in the labor room. Twenty eight of them delivered within 1–2 hours while normal delivery takes 3–4 hours or more. None of them needed any sedation or anesthesia for the labor. All the babies were born in very good condition.

Two methods of natural childbirth were compared by midwives from our hospital. They compared natural childbirth in a group of ten women in their first childbirth, who underwent preparations for childbirth and labor according to the Reed Lamage System to a group of ten women who did Paula's exercises during the active phase of labor.

Both groups were delivered by the same midwife in order to eliminate the influence of personality on the process of delivery. There was no difference in the age of the women, or their socioeconomic status.

Analysing the Freedman curve from both groups it was found that Paula's method shortened the active phase of labor by 47 minutes and 30 seconds, and the dilatation process is greater with an average of 0.4 cm per hour.

We now try to prepare the pregnant ladies from the fifth or sixth month onwards for the delivery with Paula's method. We plan to compare a group of 100 women in their first pregnancy using Paula's exercises to 100 who do not use her method.

Pathological Pregnancies (by Dr. H. Tifereth)

I tried some simple exercises in Paula's method on women with pathology in their past or in the present pregnancy and found them beneficial. For example, a lady who had uterine contractions with pain and bleeding from the 11th week of pregnancy started to do the exercise. The uterine contractions disappeared and she delivered in the 40th week. Another lady who had delivered with Caesarean section in her 30th week in her first pregnancy after a long time of hospitalisation and conventional treatment for premature contractions was seen by me in her 16th week of her second pregnancy with a very contracted uterus and with a small dilatation of the cervix of uterus. We started these exercises along with the usual treatment and after a month or two we could stop the medicines. She continued the exercises up to term and delivered a healthy girl with normal weight. After two years she gave normal birth to a third baby with the aid of these exercises.

Another good example is a lady with a twin pregnancy who delivered in the 31st week underweight babies. She came to me after 9 years. This time also she was pregnant with twins and her uterus was very contracted in the 14th week when I saw her. She started to exercise from that time onwards, and continued to work normally without any hospitalization or medication, and after the 41st week of pregnancy delivered healthy girls of normal weight.

Vaginismus   (by Dr. H. Tifereth)

Another field where I applied Paula's method is in ladies with vaginismus. Here as we all know there are involuntary contractions of the vaginal opening during intercourse. By doing Paula's exercises the lady could relax her muscles. I treated more than 20 patients with these exercises and most of these were cured within 3–4 sessions. In women who had the problem for over 2 years or had marital or personal psychic problems it took up to 7–8 sessions. Except for three ladies who had no partner at the time of treatment all reported of good sexual intercourse afterwards. The project included some cases which were unsuccessfully treated elsewhere and were referred to me to try Paula's method.

The toughest case was referred to me after two years of unsuccessful treatment by the conventional method. After that she underwent an operation to widen her vaginal opening. When this also was unsuccessful she was referred to me. After 7–8 sessions without any aid or cooperation from her partner during the treatment she succeeded to have normal intercourse.

CHAPTER 5

Pathological Conditions that Benefited by Sphincter Gymnastics

Sphincter Gymnastics is a gymnastics method. I have no pretense to cure illnesses with it. People resort to Sphincter Gymnastics, as they do to other gymnastic methods, out of a motivation to improve their general health and well-being. For the past 45 years I have taught gymnastics using the method I developed. During this time I have received reports from people who came to Sphincter Gymnastics out of the general motive mentioned, who were amazed when various maladies and pains improved or even disappeared entirely. The following chapter is based on such reports.

Children with Developmental Disturbances

Some years ago, at my request, a pediatrician, Professor Abraham Gottlieb of Tel Aviv University, put me in touch with the management of an institution in which Down's Syndrome children are sheltered. For some time, I, together with my pupils, who like myself had volunteered for this project, engaged in Sphincter Gymnastics with several of these children.

The institution's physician, Dr. Benjamin Morag, first examined the children. Then, in a short film, also made before the program started, he explained each child's condition.

The exercise and massage program went on about eight months, at an average of five times a week. We worked with each child for half an hour in a total of 157 lessons per child. We started with eight children, and added a ninth several months later.

After about three months (65 sessions) another film was made. Dr. Morag wrote a report on the children's progress, also presenting it in graph form. This medical report, covering the period from November 6, 1979 to June, 17, 1980, i.e. only 142 sessions, shows great progress in the children's condition.

In view of the experience I acquired working with children diagnosed as having Down's Syndrome, it seems to me that these children's compulsive movements are their bodies' natural need, and should therefore not be suppressed. This refers to the compulsive movements of Down's Syndrome children as well as of children with other disabilities.

For example, both autistic and Down's Syndrome children often bang their heads on the wall, In my opinion, this stems from the body's demand to help muscles that are not functioning properly. If we give them vigorous head and forehead massages, they will stop doing it and will demand the massages instead.

Such children also slam their backs against the wall, around the should blades or the small of the back. If we give them appropriate massage or certain sphincter exercises, they will calm down, will look pleased, and the compulsive movement will stop of its own accord.

When a child slams his back against the wall around the shoulder blades, it shows that the abdominal muscles, which are activated by the front sphincter, are not working well enough. It is our job to strengthen this muscle group.

Weakness of the front muscles usually makes the antagonistic muscles (i.e. the back muscles activated by the rear sphincter) work too hard. This shows up in disquiet and aggressiveness. A gentle pounding massage between the shoulder blades will quickly enable such a child to calm down, and even fall asleep easily. (Every mother is familiar with the pats on the back she uses to put her baby to sleep).

A game little children are fond of ('round round the garden...') consists of the mother's finger rubbing the child's palm. This calms a child down, because the muscles of the palm are also connected with the front sphincter.

The Down's Syndrome children who took part in the eight month Sphincter Gymnastics course of massage and exercise were found to have progressed dramatically in behavior, comprehension, appearance and level of motor coordination.

Some of them attempted to talk. Two or three began to articulate words, which had been impossible to do with a tongue that was slack, wide, and hanging outside the mouth. After exercising, most of the children could keep their tongues inside their mouths.

In those cases in which the children suffered from spastic movements, these movements disappeared almost entirely.

Once the front sphincter and the muscles linked with it were strengthened, the children became quieter, friendlier and more cooperative.

If these children are shown movements and exercises, they are eager to copy them and proud when they succeed in doing so.

The eyes of the children who took part in the gymnastics, which had been expressionless to start with, became alert and lively. Some of the children have learned to walk by themselves; others with support. All crave to, and are trying to, learn to walk.

Bed-wetting

When the reason for bed-wetting is emotional — it is a matter for a psychologist. But there are children, and even adults, who have never really been dry. Many people suffering from this condition as a result of weak muscles, including some of very advanced age, have been freed from it by simple Sphincter Gymnastics exercises.

People who wet because of muscle weakness often exhibit 'reversed breathing', i.e., breathing that pushes downward — instead of upward as in correct breathing. Sphincter Gymnastics focuses on correcting the breathing, which results in strengthening the muscles and thereby stops the bed-wetting.

With children and adults who wet because of muscle weakness, we do not usually start with exercising the front sphincter. This also applies to cases of a prolapsed rectum, bladder or vagina. Most people affected in these ways do not have enough sensation, if any, in these slack, damaged muscles.

Exercise must begin with those sphincters that are still functioning properly. Anyone can open and close their eyes to a certain extent. So eye exercise must be used to activate the lower sphincters. Through correct eye action, the lower sphincters can be restored to normal functioning.

Depression

Why do Sphincter Gymnastics have such a beneficial effect on people suffering from depression?

Depressives usually have bad posture, shoulders slumped, head very bowed, corners of the mouth pulled down. They drag their feet when they walk, treading on the entire sole and not lifting their knees. The abdomen falls forward and the back is round. They often suffer from constipation. This is a degeneration of posture resulting from faulty functioning of the sphincters.

In the course of the gymnastics, a depressive's state of mind benefits visibly as his posture improves. As the patient's physical balance is restored through exercising, his mental equilibrium improves, too. Now he knows which exercises help him regain his physical and mental balance. He has learned what he has to do for himself, without having to turn to someone else for help, to achieve physical and emotional harmony.

Speech impediments and unclear speech often improve markedly, as do nervous tics, compulsive motions and muscle spasms. In all cases, it is evident that as physical condition improves, the mental and emotional condition improves, as well.

Many reports from children, teenagers and even adults have mentioned improved powers of concentration. As a result of Sphincter Gymnastics they have been able to cope more successfully with both mental and physical tasks.

There are people who suffer from excessive sweating especially in the face and hands. On the other hand, there are those who do not perspire at all. And there are people who cry a great deal — to whom the tears always come — while others can't cry at all. Again, many reports from people who do Sphincter Gymnastics have noted great improvement and sometimes complete normalization of these conditions, which leads to the conclusion that such disturbances are associated with inadequate functioning of the sphincters.

Asthma

Asthmatics have also reported significant improvement and even complete normalization of their breathing as a result of Sphincter Gymnastics. Their reports also mention that they are now able to help themselves with Sphincter Gymnastics, whereas they had previously been dependent on medications and devices.

An asthmatic does not usually have good posture. But once he has straightened up through Sphincter Gymnastics, he almost always knows which exercise he has to do to feel better. And most important of all, he can help himself during an attack or when he doesn't feel well, without recourse to medications or someone else's assistance.

As usual, we do not start out by exercising the weak sphincter, but reach it through the healthy sphincter. People with asthma often have big toes that are turned inward. Working with the urethral sphincter is out of the question with them. (So they must not be given the Prolonged 'Sh' Exercise — see p. 158 — or any other exercise which directly affects that sphincter.)

We begin with exercises to strengthen the back muscles, and before anything else the 'Upper Lip to Nose Exercise' (see p. 153). In difficult cases the patient can't do this exercise either, and then we have to start with eyelid exercises (see p. 148). The 'Fingers to Palms Exercise' (p. 163) also has a beneficial effect on asthmatics, and so does the 'Hand on Eyes Exercise' (p. 164).

These are the exercises that treatment should usually start with. It is impossible, however, to give precise instructions, since each body reacts differently, and treatment must be suited to each case individually.

Prolapses

Various kinds of prolapses of internal abdominal organs are liable to throw a person off balance. 'Postnatal blues' may be the result of a prolapse. This may also be the cause of many cases of unhappy marriages, divorces and disturbed family lives.

Housewives or working wives — after strenuous routine work like cooking, caring for children, etc. — are often rendered incapable of thinking objectively. Up to a certain point, the lower pelvic muscles hold the uterus up. If, however, fatigue passes the permissible limit — and this limit is different for everyone — the shoulders fall forward, the lordoses at the small of the back and the neck get deeper, the uterus moves or drops (prolapses) and the result is loss of self-control. The voice gets loud and shrill and the words increasingly aggressive. When the husband comes home, also tired and edgy after a day's work, neither spouse has patience for the other or for the children. Instances of over-anxiety may quite often also be the result of general prolapse. Sphincter Gymnastics can be helpful here, too.

Flat Feet

Everybody knows what flat feet are. But not everybody knows that they can often be brought back to a normal state. To start with, Sphincter Gymnastics is used to straighten the body. This results in the fallen arch lifting and the foot gradually becoming normal. Doing the 'Close-Open Eye Exercise' (see p. 151) causes the feet themselves to begin to work and become more flexible. That is a prerequisite for correcting flat feet.

It would seem that we could achieve this by starting with front sphincter exercises. But in flat footed people this sphincter is quite often not functioning as it should. So it is preferable to begin with the oral sphincter. If the mouth is contracted, the shoulders pull back and the chest cage rises. The lordoses become flatter and the pelvis returns to a more normal position. As a result the stance of the feet also improves.

When the 'Upper Lip to Nose Exercise' (see p. 153) is done so that the curled upper lip does reach the nose, the foot also rises. The 'Fingers to Palms Exercise' (see p. 163) is also useful for improving the state of the feet.

When the lower lip is contracted as in drinking (see p. 24) or when both lips are contracted, the feet begin to arch. They arch up with each contraction of the lips, and sink back with each relaxation.

The sphincter muscles must be strengthened in order to get flat feet into proper shape.

Varicose Veins

In his book, *The Pathology and Therapy of Breathing* (p. 21), Prof. Ludwig Hofbauer writes: "During inhalation the veins of the lower body inflate and the veins of the upper body deflate, and conversely, during exhalation the veins of the upper body inflate, and those of the lower body deflate..."

When the breathing is short and/or shallow, the blood cannot flow back from the veins of the legs. It accumulates, and varicose veins are often the result.

In states of fatigue, anger, excitement, fear and depression — it is the breathing that suffers first of all.

When the legs hurt very much as happens to housewives and other people whose work entails prolonged standing, some time should be allocated after work to doing the following exercise: lie on the back on a flat surface, lift the knees to the chest as far as is individually possible, place hands on knees (if possible), and emit a drawn out quiet 'sh' sound (see p. 158) for as long as one's breath holds out. As a result, breathing becomes calmer, longer and deeper.

People of an advanced age may plant their feet on a flat surface with the knees bent instead of gathered up to the chest. It is also possible to prop the head up with a flat pillow, which may often be dispensed with later. It all depends on the state of health and age.

Hemorrhoids

Hemorrhoids are accumulations of blood in the veins of the rectum. What has been said above about varicose veins also applies to hemorrhoids. Exhalations are not long enough. Short exhalations can not support the spine and do not enable the blood in the veins of the lower body to flow back sufficiently. Long exhalations activate the abdominal muscles and support the spine. In contrast, short exhalations increase the lordosis at the small of the back. The abdominal muscles do not contract sufficiently and so do not give proper support to the spine and the contents of the abdomen. The edges of the upper pelvis tilt forward and so do the contents of the abdomen, producing increased lordosis at the small of the back and the neck.

When lying on the back with knees either drawn up to the chest or just bent, and uttering a 'sh' sound as long as possible (see p. 158), the lordoses — if they are not too deep — are usually first of all flattened, the lower sphincters are able to contract and relax, and the blood in the veins to flow back. This obviously affects hemorrhoids which, as stated, are accumulations of blood in the veins. The shrinking of the hemorrhoids occurs very slowly, so the exercise should be kept up for a long time.

Ageing

Shaking and trembling of the head and/or limbs in old people (not Parkinson's disease) sometimes stems from faulty action of the oral sphincter and the lower sphincters. In consequence, the other sphincters and muscles are no longer under control either. This is a very depressing condition for the aged. Reports of old people who have done Sphincter Gymnastics suggest that there are certain easy-to-perform exercises by means of which it is often possible to restore the affected muscles to more or less competent action.

Old people cough often. Coughing pushes the diaphragm down and keeps the lower sphincters and the oral sphincter from working properly, which causes loss of control over them. This generates other disabilities — emotional and physical — such as weakening of the memory and difficulty in walking. The eyes also are affected, as are physical posture and mental stability.

This is a state in which the mouth usually remains open. It should be mentioned in passing that one often sees young adults, and even children, who keep their mouths open. Because of the gaping mouth, most of these individuals are unable to think and concentrate properly, and are very forgetful. In addition, the ears, the eyes, the nose and the lower sphincters are also not working properly. This is reflected both in posture and behavior.

In such cases, good results may be obtained when better sphincter activity is induced by Sphincter Gymnastics.

PART II
CASE HISTORIES

Sphincter Gymnastics is a gymnastics system and as such is intended — as has already been indicated — to bring about an improvement in the well-being and general health of those who engage in it. In many cases, people who practiced Sphincter Gymnastics have noted improvement or even complete relief from ailments and pains from which they had been suffering. During the many years I have worked with Sphincter Gymnastics, word has spread of my method's beneficial effect on many ailments and pains. Moreover, it has also come to the attention of physicians, many of whom have referred patients to me and continue to do so. It goes without saying that such referrals are accepted willingly and without examination of their motives. The only thing I always and in all cases require is medical confirmation that the applicant's health will permit him or her to engage in Sphincter Gymnastics.

The cases described below are examples. The facts are accurate, but the names are of course fictitious. The real names are on record in my files.

As the manner of rehabilitation is individual — so too the manner of reporting differs from one case to the next. Almost all the reports are quoted verbatim, without editing of style or content.

Shulamit — Arthritis

I was born in 1945. At an early age I was found to have rheumatoid arthritis and a deficiency in thrombocytes. In 1959 following a steep drop in my thrombocyte count, my spleen was removed. The count has since remained normal.

Until the birth of my child in 1969, my condition was more or less static, with recurring pain in all joints of the body and slight deformations of the fingers. After the delivery, severe inflammation of the joints set in, especially on the right side. Two years later I underwent two operations on the palm of my hand. In 1972 I gave birth to a second child. At the end of 1973, I came down with a bad case of pneumonia. About a year later I fell ill again with an unidentified inflammatory ailment and a lack of leucocytes. Because of this, I stopped taking medications.

Early in 1976 I suffered an extremely severe attack of meningitis, accompanied by paralysis of the right half of my face, and a great deal of damage to the joints, especially the hip joints. For a time I could not walk at all. Later I did walk for a few months, though very little and with a bad limp. After that I was confined to a wheelchair, the condition of my hip joints — especially on the left side — deteriorating steadily.

In December 1977 I was operated on and my left hip joint replaced. During the two years that elapsed between the meningitis and the operation I hardly used my legs at all, and of course the muscles had atrophied badly. After the operation I began to get about with crutches. I came to Paula Garbourg about five months later, still on crutches, treading mainly on my right foot. The left foot was very weak and by no means able to carry my weight.

My face still showed marked signs of paralysis. The right side was slack, and lip movement on that side — both contracting and opening — was very limited. The right eye did not close completely, and the contraction of the eyebrow was very weak. The left side was contracted, the left eyebrow low, the eye small and the lip very constricted.

I began to work with Paula Garbourg on activating the sphincter muscles. The immediate response was amazing. The muscles of my hand and feet — muscles I could hardly remember existed — began to function independently. The visible results were very marked indeed. My walk improved immeasurably. Within two weeks I got rid of the crutches. I used a cane for a while, but got rid of it too.

There was vast improvement in my face as well. The contracted left side relaxed. Lip movements on the right side became broader and the asymmetry began disappearing.

I have kept up the exercises since May of 1978. Of course the progress has slowed down, but it continues all the time. I now walk without a cane, with a mild limp due to the condition of my right hip joint. My left leg has become unrecognizably stronger, and far more mobile. The freedom of movement of my feet, which was most limited before, has increased. My ability to use my hands has increased. And what is most interesting is that the more I exercise, the more the general condition of my joints benefit and conversely — when I work less, the pains get worse again.

Sima — Arthritis

I came to Paula depressed and in pain, almost beyond desperation after a great many physiotherapy treatments had failed to do me any good. I decided to try her method because in my extremity I was ready for anything, just so as not to give in to total despair. And this time luck was on my side.

I had the kind of arthritis that conventional medicine defines as chronic. To my misfortune the disease attacked almost every part of my body, especially the knees, which were so swollen, red and fevered that I could not move them.

After a year of total confinement to bed, most of the muscles of my body had of course atrophied, and I couldn't climb even a single step or go to the bathroom.

Paula immediately began a series of exercises, and in that first lesson I already felt some relief.

I felt she was really going to help me, so I buckled down to the hard labor she imposed on me. It's difficult to explain exactly why it was so backbreakingly hard, since the exercises appear quite easy at first sight. But I remember that I used to come home dead tired and in need of a lot of sleep and rest.

The real relief began to appear after a few lessons. My body responded and started to put itself to work. The more my state of mind improved, the more my overall physical feeling improved. The knee still ached, but I was already able to get to Paula's place on my own and without a cane.

I am not enough of an expert on the body's secrets and it is hard for me to explain what happened during the exercises, but one thing is clear: my tired, atrophied body is starting to show signs of life. It is beginning to function and to channel vitality into all sorts of deteriorated places that had stopped responding, and were to all intents and purposes dead for such a long time. At the same time, a great new energy has started flowing through my veins. The tiredness has made way for tremendous strength and energy and an enormous capacity to do all kinds of things, as though the body wanted to make up for the time lost when it was ill.

I still have to keep exercising, but today I am capable of doing so on my own at home. After five years of total dependence on my family, my husband and my four children, I am now capable of taking care of them all, working outdoors, hoeing in the garden, and taking part in marches and excursions. It is a priceless achievement.

Netiva — Arthritis

This is the book that saved me. I suffered from arthritic pains which resulted from intensive writing (agonised writing – someone told me), and for 7 years I didn't touch my guitar, which was for me a terrible loss.

As a result of the radio programs of Rachel Halfi on Paula Garbourg, I bought the book, started to exercise myself, and a miracle happened I returned to the guitar, and I already again can play Bach's Chaconne.

I exercise according to the book for 10 minutes every morning at dawn (it helps me get over the news), and for about another half hour during the day, and there isn't a day when I don't say – Thank Good that you sent me this book and this woman – Paula Garbourg.

David — Lumbago

On August 16, 1968 I suffered an attack of acute pain in the region of the lower back and hips, which radiated strongly to my left leg. I couldn't walk, sit or stand, and the pain didn't subside when I was lying down, either. In this condition I consulted an orthopedist, who diagnosed 'a severe attack of lumbago, with extreme rigidity in the lumbar region'. He prescribed a course of medication and instructed me to stay in bed. When two weeks had gone by without any improvement, he suggested a plaster cast for the pelvis and informed me that if this did not help either, surgery would be required. It was in this state that I turned to Mrs Paula Garbourg, who started treating me with exercises following her special method. After only a few treatments with her, my condition improved enough to enable me to get up myself and travel to her place to do the exercises. My condition kept improving gradually and after about six weeks of daily exercise with Mrs. Garbourg I was as strong as ever and went back to work.

It seems to me that I can sum up the treatment I went through with Mrs. Garbourg as a process of physical re-education, in which I learned to use my body correctly and effectively, and to perform any action without any restrictions, in the right way.

I must mention the preventive character of this education, thanks to which I have been spared recurring attacks of lumbago despite the orthopedist's verdict that I should expect such recurrences. I am glad to say that despite that forecast and although I do not limit my physical activities in any way. I have not had a single serious attack. In the isolated instances when I had had mild backaches, I have overcome them in short order by using the exercises I learned with Mrs. Paula Garbourg.

It goes without saying that I owe a debt of gratitude to Mrs. Garbourg for her treatment, and am happy to have had the opportunity to learn from her.

Amos — Backaches

Every year since about 1975, seasonal changes in the weather brought severe attacks of pain in my lower back, and sometimes in my right shoulder as well. I went to doctors, who tried to help me with stretching (in a physiotherapy clinic) and gave me shots and pills. I went to specialists in massage, acupuncture and exercise — but all I got from them, sometimes, was temporary relief that only lasted until the next change in weather. Things got worse in 1979 when the backaches began to spread to my legs, and the shoulder pains to my right arm and hand, making it hard to write, I also began to feel a tingling sensation, like selzer water bubbling, in my hand.

My treatment with Paula began, I think, in October or November 1979. Paula started with a thorough review of my history of illnesses and injuries, and observation of how I stood, sat and walked. She was not like the doctors, who were only interested in the X-ray pictures and assumed that defects in the vertebrae and the discs between them were the source of all my pains. In a way that surprised me greatly, Paula stated that deformations of the spine that had been found were likely to be not merely the reason for, but perhaps primarily the result of improper use of the muscles. The remedy, she said, should be sought in correct use of the muscles, especially the abdominal muscles, to rebalance the spine and restore it to proper posture and action.

Paula also added that it might well be that the action of the muscles was being hampered by wounds from the War of Independence, which had left deep scars in my back, under my right shoulder, and in my left leg. The general purpose of the treatment was defined as being to strengthen muscles that had become slack or had been injured, so as to bring the entire body back to correct posture and movement.

Improvement was evident after about a week, when the pains began receding gradually from the extremities to the center — until they disappeared altogether. To start with, the 'bubbling' in my right hand got weaker and then stopped. Soon after, the pains in my legs began to dwindle and go away. Then the shoulder pains proceeded to become weaker. And only at the end, after quite a few weeks (I think it was about three months), did the backaches stop as well.

At first I came to lessons at Paula's institute about four times a week, and worked 2–3 hours each time. Little by little I cut down the number of days and the number of hours per day. After about six weeks I stopped going to the institute, and carried on alone at home about an hour a day.

Doing the exercises induced incidental activation of other muscle groups, like ripples spreading in a pond, and a sense of liberation in other parts of the body. In fact my body itself began to 'talk' and to activate all sorts of muscles and members in ways that surprised even me. For instance, one exercise induced contractions and relaxations that paralleled those of the lower abdominal muscles — in the palms, fingers, soles and toes — as well as contracting and relaxing the mouth, the eyes and even the ears. An eye exercise generated tongue movements parallel to those of the eyes, and then leg movements that generated rocking of the pelvis. It was as though my whole body was dancing like a marionette operated by strings being pulled by the eyes.

The scars on my back and leg, which over the years had become colorless and numb like dead skin, regained a living color and began to develop sensitivity. They started to fill out with new flesh at the edges, as though they were again joining in the body's general activity.

All in all, there also came an overall feeling as though my body had become lighter and all its members were functioning more harmoniously. Both walking and standing, which had been particularly difficult before, became easier and more coordinated.

As I understand it, Paula has a whole philosophy she bases her techniques on. Unfortunately I didn't manage to go into her views deeply, mainly because there wasn't time for detailed discussions beyond the exercise instructions and the follow-up. The little I do understand comes from an article by Naomi

Shemer (one of Israel's leading song writers) which was very important and enlightening for me to read, and from talks with assistants who often sat in the room while I exercised.

In August 1980 I traveled to the U.S. with my family. Under the burden, first of the preparations for the trip, and then of my work, and because it seemed to me I was completely cured of my backaches, I neglected the exercises for several months. The results were not long in coming. When the weather changed drastically at the beginning of December I had a new, severe attack of backaches. They were not as painful or widespread as they had been before working with Paula — it seemed something had remained from the exercises. I went back to work on them an hour and a half a day at first, coming down to half or three quarters of an hour as I got better. It seems to me the process of recovery was faster this time. My body, which already knew the exercises, again 'took the initiative' and from time to time I could feel it 'talking to itself' as it were, during exercise sessions, leading me to do some experimenting of my own, and fixing specific times and levels for each exercise.

Nora — Backaches

In February 1978 a neurologist referred me to Mrs. Garbourg's institute. I had been told by the doctor that I had two options. One was to undergo another operation on my back, the other — to start a course of treatment by the Garbourg method. I chose the latter. Here I must relate the train of events that led up to this choice.

In 1971 I gave birth to my first son. The delivery was normal, but prolonged and painful. Afterwards I began to suffer from severe backaches, which became worse as time went by.

Absolute rest, painkillers, and chiropractic treatment did no good. Two years later it was determined that the pains were caused by a slipped disc. All treatment efforts came to nothing. They included injections in the spinal cord and adjoining muscles. The result: an allergy to medications and sedatives. In the course of time a serious infection developed in the sciatic nerve leading down into the left leg, as well as a degeneration of the muscles in that leg and loss of sensation in its toes. The deterioration of my condition obliged the doctors to operate on me, and two discs were removed. The relief was concrete, but I was still restricted.

After another baby my back got worse, I lost sensation of my left leg and similar symptoms began to appear in the right. Life became hell again. I wouldn't hear of another operation! My mood was terrible and that made my physical condition even worse. Here I was with a small child and an infant, and incapable of functioning as a mother.

Now I'll come back to where I started my story. Right at the beginning of treatment, Mrs. Garbourg explained her therapeutic method to me: a very simple and very, very logical method. In the first sessions I did only the simplest of things, like the simple movement we make every few moments — blinking the eyes. But it seems this movement is capable of relieving pain. At first it was hard to do even this, but as the number of sessions increased I was able to ease a bit of the pain with the aid of the blinking exercises, and other simple facial exercises which would appear to have nothing to do with the back. The feeling came back in my right leg, but only partially in the left.

By means of simple everyday movements and simple exercises I have been able — when the pain was at its very worst — to ease it myself and to function as a person. Besides that, Mrs. Garbourg has taught me how to perform day-to-day actions, like caring for a baby, in a way that doesn't hurt or strain the back unnecessarily.

All the time I was undergoing treatment with Paula I was under medical surveillance, and there has been some improvement from a medical standpoint. For example, in my first neurological examination after giving birth, the angle through which I could move my left foot was only 15–20°, while after three months of treatment it had gone up to 30–35°, in my case a very considerable gain. I could also bend my back again.

By means of breathing exercises I have been able to control the pains that used to grip me, and to function again. At the present stage, this treatment has removed the threat of the surgeon's scalpel and I hope that threat has been removed for good.

Avinoam — Infantile Paralysis

I contracted polio when I was half a year old. The disease left me with two totally paralyzed legs, and a left arm paralyzed in the muscle that lifts the hand. To walk, I used a pair of orthopedic fittings for the legs, as well as long crutches that reached the armpits.

Throughout my childhood I was under constant treatment by excellent orthopedic surgeons. I did my best for years without much success. As the years went by it became clear to the doctors and was even explained to me with the utmost delicacy that there was no chance of any improvement whatsoever in my condition in the future. In the doctor's opinion the only existing way to make things easier for me was to engage in sports and physical activity to strengthen the remaining muscles, to compensate or substitute for those that would never be able to function again.

And so, at the age of 18 I embarked on intensive physical

activity aimed at improving my physical condition. Among other things, this activity included swimming, wheelchair basketball and fencing.

I felt that the healthy part of my body was getting stronger but the paralyzed part was staying the same. And the imbalance between the healthy limbs and the paralyzed ones was getting more pronounced. When I swam I used to bring the paralyzed hand forward with the assistance of the healthy one. The legs took no part in swimming, but dragged behind the body. I managed to walk by means of jumps and thrusts of the legs.

After two years of this kind of activity, I found out about a special kind of gymnastics method given by Mrs. Paula Garbourg.

I came to Mrs. Garbourg's house out of sheer curiosity as I didn't believe there was still something to do that I hadn't done yet. But I felt I owed it to myself to try anything that offered a spark of hope for improving my condition.

I began to exercise following Mrs. Garbourg's guidelines. Since at that time I didn't understand what the exercises meant, they seemed odd and useless to me. This was not the kind of gymnastics I was accustomed to but I decided to try it for a limited time.

After about a month of exercising I began to feel that *my body didn't consist of two parts — one healthy and one paralyzed — but was beginning to act as a single homogeneous unit.* The left hand and both paralyzed legs started sharing in the body's overall activity. This participation was passive and invisible at first, but I would feel it after the lesson, when I would be walking home and suddenly sense waves of heat spreading through my legs and warming key areas like the knees, etc.

In time, this began to be more active. Muscles that had for years been defined by the best of doctors as zero-level dead muscles began to flutter and contract.

Of course this activity had an immediate effect on my external appearance. My posture became erect and my walk more natural, as I had stopped thrusting my feet forward for momentum. My left shoulder got broader since the shoulder muscle, which had been totally paralyzed, began to wake up and reached a level of strength of 2–3.

When I swam in the pool, I felt a drastic change for the better. In the breast stroke I didn't have to pull my left hand forward with the right any more, since the left arm's recovering muscle succeeded in stretching the hand forward under its own power. I even succeeded in lifting my left arm out of the water while swimming the crawl, which I had not been able to accomplish before.

My surprise knew no bounds when I discovered that I could actually walk along the bottom of the pool, whereas previously my legs had floated in the water without my being able to control them at all.

After a further period of activity, I threw away my old crutches, and started using shorter ones, attached to my wrists. I also shortened the brace on my left leg, as it had strengthened considerably.

All this time I was trying to interest medical circles in what was happening in my body, so as to obtain monetary aid for my sustenance and be able to devote all my free time to exercising. I am sorry to say that I did not succeed in interesting any medical authority in taking me under its auspices. I was therefore obliged, after two years of considerable progress, to go back to my work and my studies in accountancy. As a result, my physical exercise has dwindled considerably.

Today I am married and the father of two. Comparing my physical condition before and after I began exercising with Mrs. Paula Garbourg's method, and examining the considerable progress I have achieved, which makes its mark in my daily life, I thank God for having granted it to me to learn to know my body and to improve it. On the other hand, I feel that if this method were accorded suitable recognition and assistance, I would be able to invest more time in it, and to achieve impressive results in rehabilitating most of the affected muscles.

Oren — Cerebral Palsy

(As told by his mother)
Oren was born with the umbilical cord wrapped around his neck, and was late in starting to breathe. He was in the hospital's Premature Unit about five and a half weeks, a week of that in an incubator. The diagnosis was C.P. (Cerebral Palsy). At about ten months, he began to receive physiotherapy. At the age of four he underwent a series of operations on his legs to free the tendons. The first operation was at the crotch, the next two behind the knees, and another on an ankle (Achilles tendon). After he recovered from these operations, he was fitted with leg braces, and after prolonged physiotherapy began to walk with crutches. When he was about eight years old, Oren stopped using the crutches, and began to walk freely.

It is the right half of Oren's body that is most badly affected: severe damage in the right eye, from which he can hardly see at all, and pronounced damage in the right arm and right leg. The damage on the left side is milder, which produced an asymmetry in his facial expression, body and movements, and serious problems of equilibrium and balance in walking.

That was the condition Oren was in when he cam to the Garbourg Institute.

He was under treatment for eight months, intensive to start with (about 4–5 times a week), and later coming down to twice a week — until we moved from Tel Aviv to Katzrin.

As a result of the treatments, a marked improvement has been apparent in his balance when walking.

His facial expression has become more symmetrical.

He has gained better control of his hands, which shows particularly in his handwriting having become much more regular and organized.

Dorothy — Brain Damage

Born November 21, 1952 in a difficult labor and as a breech baby. During birth I suffered brain damage to the motor area, Cerebral Palsy with spastic athetosis, mostly on the left side of my body, left arm and shoulder, and mainly in the head and mouth.

My left foot was pigeon-toed. I wore a brace on calf and foot to straighten the foot. It did not help. I had muscle transplant surgery in my left foot at age six. As a result, I am no longer pigeon-toed.

I first noticed arthetoid movements in my left shoulder and hand after the foot operation.

At age 10 my left hip became dislocated due to the strain of carrying a heavy schoolbag with books on my left side. I had an operation (age 11) to put the hip bone back into the socket. While recuperating, I used two crutches, then only one later, on the right side, due to doctor's orders. As a result, I developed a strain on the upper right side of my back, and scoliosis occurred. My hip muscles on the left side have never healed properly enough for them to hold my hip bone in the socket, so the top of my femur kept popping in and out of the socket whenever I walked — and my back pulled to the other side at the same time. It was very painful to walk, and as a result of the pain, my spastic athetoid movements became worse.

I wore a back brace for about two years to correct my balance. It was very painful. This did not correct the problem in my hip, but aided me to walk straighter while I was wearing the brace.

At age $17^1/_2$ I had an operation — hip fusion; and at age 18 — Baker's Release of the left tendon on the left foot (ankle) was performed. This improved my balance and ability to walk, but my athetoid movements were the same. I practiced yoga for a few years. This strengthened my whole body and helped the pains in my lower back. Chiropractic treatments also helped the pain and the stiffness in my body, but athetoid movements in my head and hands were the same.

I found Paula Garbourg at age $25^1/_2$. Through her exercises I achieved immediate improvements in coordination of my hands, head, mouth and in my ability to move my hips freely when I walk. The athetoid movements in my left shoulder decreased to the point where I hardly even have them now. My back straightened considerably when I walk. I now have more energy and a general feeling of relaxation in my entire body, thanks to Paula, which I never had before in my life. Also, my left hand opened for the first time in my life.

Friends and acquaintances who have seen me after a few months or a year commented (without my asking them) that my general coordination and head and hand movements have improved enormously, and that I seem much calmer physically. Even people who were not at all aware of the fact that I have been doing any kind of physical therapy have commented on how much more coordination I have.

Another thing — I could never wear flat shoes before (which are better for my back) because my left foot used to hurt too much when it was flat. Now, I almost always wear flat shoes with no problems, because since I have been doing the exercises, my foot straightened itself out to the point where it is more comfortable to wear flat shoes, thanks to Paula.

Also, before starting Paula's program, my mouth used to twitch uncontrollably to the right, especially the right side of my upper lip. This was a very prominent feature in my face, and obvious from the moment someone first looked at me. The whole mouth was tilted to the right, was almost always twitching, and all in all was always very, very tense. These characteristics have almost completely disappeared since I have been doing Paula's exercises. My mouth is straight, and one can hardly see any signs of irregularities about it any more.

Another thing that improved tremendously with the exercises was the chronic bladder problem I have always had. Sometimes for months at a time, I have found it difficult to control my sudden urge to urinate, and have had a few accidents and many, many near accidents over the years. I have been to several doctors who have been able to do nothing, and tests showed nothing. Now that I've been doing Paula's exercises, the bladder problem has almost completely disappeared. Thanks to Paula again.

I have started to use my left hand much more. Before the exercises, I had to force myself to use my left hand, and even when I did, it was usually too tight and shaky to be very functional. Now I don't have to think about using it. It often starts to work of its own accord, is much less shaky and tight, and is often completely relaxed, something that never used to happen.

Mira — Handicapped from Birth

(Doctor's testimony)
Mira is a 16-year old girl. She was referred to the Garbourg Institute by the neurologist who was treating her.

She was born handicapped with a short, paralyzed palate and a defective vocal cord. She had plastic surgery on the palate and a further operation to correct cross-eyedness.

Following the surgical intervention she began to suffer from acute headaches and eye pains. Breathing difficulties appeared, and a strangling sensation that interfered with her falling asleep. She suffered from chronic fatigue and sensitivity that caused various nose, ear and throat disorders during the winter months.

With the aid of Sphincter Gymnastics, she learned how to overcome the strangling feeling. There was immediate improvement in her ability to sleep. Her constant fatigue disappeared, and in the course of treatment the inflammatory winter ailments stopped. Her ability to function in studies and in work has increased.

Ilan — Vocal Cord Problems

(A letter)

I came to Mrs. Garbourg for treatment four years ago. My problem was with my voice. I had suffered from it even before adolescence and also afterwards, when the voice usually changes. I spoke in a high register, and with an excessively singsong intonation. I also suffered from frequent hoarseness.

I asked several physicians for help, among them a specialist in voice and communication problems. I received fatiguing but fruitless treatment from him.

Among the medical advice I received was a reference to psychiatric therapy — which I declined. At the next stage I reached a hormone specialist. His tests showed my hormones to be in a completely normal state.

In my further search for a solution to my problem I came upon a physician-graphologist, who referred me to Mrs. Garbourg.

The treatment was brief, six months all told. Paula demanded that I be meticulous and punctual. And indeed, the results were not long in coming. I now speak in a deep and manly tone. Attacks of hoarseness have stopped bothering me. Other changes have taken place too. My head, which usually tilted to the right, has stopped doing so. My personal confidence has been reinforced and my sexual performance has increased immeasurably.

I thank Paula — an energetic and diligent woman with an amazing creative joy. In practice, she remodels desperate people and is happy in their success.

Dror — Nose Problems

For me, Paula is a chapter in my life, a turning point in my self awareness that came to me inadvertently. I met Paula when I was 24, in 1957, right after my wife, Ruthie, had started treatment.

Ruthie, who had recovered from polio with a crippled right leg, had undergone physiotherapy that helped her. We reached Paula afterwards. Ruthie was skeptical about the treatment, since she was used to another kind. Paula, with her great perceptiveness, sensed this and asked us to be patient for two weeks. And sure enough, within two weeks surprising changes started taking place in Ruthie's ability to control and employ her body.

Very curious, I escorted Ruthie to her lessons and even waited while they were in progress. That's how I met and made friends with Paula. I told Paula that I suffered from nose and breathing problems, having been operated on three times when I was in the army, to expand a left nostril that was virtually closed and move a septum that was too close to the eye. The operations had not turned out well. I developed great sensitivity to certain smells, with intense sneezing and an almost chronic running nose. Another thing that bothered me was a sharp pain below the left shoulder whenever I rode my bicycle for more than five minutes.

When I talked about this with Paula, she asked me to open my mouth and lift my head. On the right side of my upper jaw the first pre-molar tooth was out of line with the other teeth, growing inwards into my mouth. Paula realized I had developed the habit of pushing my tongue up against this tooth. In her opinion this pressure bent the palate and made the septum above it deviate to the left. She suggested that I have the out-of-line tooth treated,

84

and immediately start pressing my tongue against the opposite (i.e., the left) side of the palate. Within a comparatively short time I began to feel my left nostril expanding. The sensitivity in my nose was decreasing and to my surprise the pain under my left shoulder was disappearing, too.

In lessons, I wore only a T-shirt and tennis shorts, though I started in wintertime. In the course of a lesson I would be lying down, and afterwards even sitting up or standing. But I was working hard with my whole body, and I never felt any need to turn on the heater. On the contrary, I usually even asked to have a window opened. After the first lessons, I sometimes felt muscle pains, as though I had been doing the most strenuous of exercises, when I actually hadn't moved at all.

Paula never told me to straighten up, to stand erect or to perform any action with my body. The actions were all done by the facial and respiratory muscles, and took the body by surprise.

I remember being asked to lie on my stomach and do a lip exercise. I found myself lying only on the middle of my abdomen while my head, chest, hands and legs were pulling upwards in such a high arch — that I would certainly never have been capable of getting half as high with an effort of the body muscles alone.

When asked to stand and 'look' at my right (or left) ear — after a few minutes of exercising and encouragement from Paula I found the upper part of my body turned in the direction of the 'looking' in a backward turn I would never have been able to accomplish with an ordinary effort of the muscles. And here the turn had been made with the body completely loose and without any effort.

In another amazing exercise I was asked to close my eyes while standing and to press hard with my eyelids. After a few minutes of work, I felt myself rising lightly to my tiptoes with my body drawn upwards in an arch. I had never before succeeded in rising so high on my tiptoes, and this was without any sense of effort in body or legs.

In the course of many years, on difficult hikes and particularly when mountain-climbing with a back-pack, I have used those 'back closures' with which the muscles of the buttocks are activated, and the effort has become much easier and simpler.

Twenty-five years have passed since then, and when I get tired while driving, when I have trouble standing for a long time, and in many other situations in which I need relaxation, release and rest on short order — I still use the exercises I learned from Paula, which have become a treasure that I unfortunately make use of too seldom.

Ahuva — Prolapse of the Uterus

I came to Paula at the age of 55 in a weakened state, having difficulty functioning in my household. I underwent tests in a hospital where I was confined to bed for 10 days under suspicion that something was wrong with my heart. The tests did not show any illness. Before treatment with Paula I was examined by a doctor. He found a severe prolapse of abdomen and everything in it. It was causing weakness, a big loss of weight, and acute pains in my abdomen and a lot of other places in my body. After some time in treatment I began to feel very much better. I gained weight. Everything returned to where it belonged and my smile came back. I am now 77 years old. I always remember Paula with the grateful feeling that she saved me from deterioration in my health that might have gone who knows how far.

Ilana — Prolapse of the Uterus

I was born in 1929, and am the mother of 3 children. All three births were normal.

A. Two years ago I began to notice unusual things that disturbed me somewhat, like the need to urinate more often than usual, and wetting myself when I coughed, sneezed or ran. After examining me, the gynecologist stated that my uterus had prolapsed a little — a first degree prolapse about which nothing could be done yet except to be patient. The months went by, and these things kept bothering me. I also felt a change in the state of my abdomen — a sort of heaviness I had not felt before. I was again examined by the same doctor and was again told that the prolapse had not yet 'progressed' and so it was impossible to operate and raise the uterus.

I came out of that visit depressed. I understood that the situation was liable to go on for a long time without my being able to correct it. This upset me emotionally.

One day, while talking to a friend, I told her about it. She dissuaded me on the spot from placing my hopes in having an operation, and offered to introduce me to a friend of hers who had developed a series of exercises by means of which the slackened muscles of the uterus could be activated to lift it along 'do it yourself' lines.

Depressed as I was, I listened attentively, and because it sounded logical and believing that my friend was endowed with a good portion of common sense — I was persuaded to take her advice and accompanied her to that woman's institute.

B. And indeed, a new page in my life was opened. The woman who had the institute looked at my face as though she was reading an open book about the state of my prolapsed uterus, briefly interrogated me about my general state of health, and agreed to accept me, provided I brought a letter from the same doctor stating that he did not object to my exercising.

Armed with the required note, I began to spend about an hour every day at the Institute, doing exercises under her guidance. I'll admit that for the first few days I didn't feel any change in my body, either while doing the exercises or afterwards. Still I wasn't discouraged. I kept coming to the Institute and following instructions. I felt I was in good hands. And sure enough, towards the end of the first week, while doing an exercise that requires a long exhalation, I suddenly felt something happening in the lower part of my abdomen. It was the beginning of things starting to happen — the muscles were pulling upwards. From that point on, the exercises were almost invariably accompanied by a distinct sense of the muscles inside my abdomen pulling upwards. This motivated me to keep doing the exercises every day at home too.

After three weeks during which I exercised almost daily, about an hour at the Institute and half an hour at home, the wetting stopped almost altogether. I wasn't afraid to run or exert myself physically any more, and no longer felt the downward push in my abdomen. I kept exercising at the same rate for another two weeks at the Institute (making five weeks in all), and since then have continued at home without supervision, faithfully and with satisfaction and a feeling of success.

C. I'm glad to say, that besides solving my main problem, the prolapsed uterus, I have enjoyed several side effects which are:

1. My memory has sharpened somewhat, I think as a result of the deep breathing.

2. My facial coloring has improved; my cheeks have turned pink.

3. My short-sightedness has diminished as a result of exercises that strengthened the eye muscles.

One might say my general appearance has improved; it has been noticed by relatives and people who know me well.

I was sorry about one thing — having to give up the high heeled shoes I liked wearing so much.

Pnina — Rehabilitation after Road Accident

(Doctor's report)

Was in a serious road accident abroad at age 25. Sustained a fracture of the sacrum, with damaged sensation in buttocks and genitals, fractures of right ankle and shin, and further injuries to left tendons and skin.

Received first aid in the country in which she was injured, and also underwent surgery there. Following some improvement in general condition, was flown back to Israel and hospitalized here for further treatment. The plaster cast was gradually removed from her leg, but she still suffered from lack of sensation and impaired bladder and bowel control. Was released from hospital in this condition and began treatment lasting about seven months at the Paula Garbourg Institute.

At the start of treatment, it was still hard for her to walk, she dragged her right leg, her face was wrinkled, her emotional state was very low, and she was suffering from a severe decline of sensation in her buttocks, right thigh, and genital area. She had stopped reading and drawing — hobbies she had engaged in a great deal.

After two months of treatment, she began to control bladder

and bowel movements. Her external appearance improved and the depression passed. Her walking improved, and a few months later she regained feeling in her genitals. Today Pnina is not limited in any way, and lives and functions perfectly normally. A few weeks ago I received a letter from her relating that she is again having a good time abroad and is even skiing. She has gone back to reading and drawing with even greater success than before the accident — and is now completing her Master's studies.

Elisheva — Rehabilitation after Road Accident

I reached Paula Garbourg's Institute early in 1977, four months after a road accident. A car had hit me from behind, injuring my back, my head and my legs. As a result, I wasn't able to turn my head to the right or the left. I couldn't walk; every few steps I had to sit down because of the very severe pains in my back and legs. I couldn't stand up for more than a few minutes. The pain was sustained and constant, stopping only when I sat or lay down.

Three years before the accident, I had started having leg pains due to changes in the spinal column which also caused a mild malformation of the pelvis.

In the first lesson I lay on the couch and, following Paula's instructions, began 'to contract and relax the eyes'. Such a simple sentence, and so fateful for me.

After a while, I began to feel very comfortable and to sense my body starting to loosen up more and more. Then I did another exercise — and the loosening up of my body got even greater.

At the end of the lesson I stood up feeling something good had happened to me, and my pain had eased a little. That feeling recurred after every single lesson. Suddenly, a few weeks later, my back and leg started aching again in the worst way. I was very frightened and downhearted.

When I got to the Institute, Paula reassured me saying this was 'a dip before the climb.'

The pains persisted and got even worse. I was a little discouraged and a little afraid but kept working constantly. I felt all sorts of changes in my body accompanied by pain in various places besides my back and legs.

I noticed the pains stopped while doing exercises, and came back only several hours later. I understood I could control the situation, count on myself and help myself.

Today, two years after the accident, I have not stopped exercising. Something new and good happens in my body every day. I have an erect posture, and can go to work, take hikes, and enjoy myself — am living a new and self-renewing life. I'm no longer afraid of the pains that are sometimes brought on by changes in the weather or by overfatigue after a long day's work. I have learned to rely on myself with the aid of these same exercises.

Aviva — Rehabilitation after Road Accident

I came to Paula in December 1978.

In 1974 I was injured in a road accident, and sustained fractures of the pelvis. I recovered in a year, coming out with no disability. A year and a half later there appeared a distressing pressure on the back of my neck.

I looked for a cure: through a sick-fund doctor (who provided me with a lot of Muscol tablets and her good advice — to get married quickly, which would reduce the pressure on my neck), by sick-fund physiotherapy, and by gymnastics that kept me agile but didn't relieve the pressure. At that time I noticed that there was a sort of small bump on the back of my neck.

With that same distressing pressure on the back of my neck — which bothered me very much — I arrived at Paula's.

After two months of intensive gymnastics by the Paula Garbourg method, I saw distinct changes in my body. Before, when lying on my back I had felt points of encounter with the floor. But I never understood what it means 'to feel all of your back on the floor'. Two months later — a new sensation — a new back!.

The pressure on my neck remained, but I had more energy and general vitality. It was easier for me to get through the day with all its duties — studies and work. I managed to do a tremendous amount, and had no trouble getting up in the morning (a real revolution for me!).

After half a year of gymnastics with Paula I became an adherent of this method, because I felt it gave me a great deal of strength and optimism and was changing my life. Paula explained to me (though not right away) that I had a condition called 'prolapse' which is caused by slack abdominal muscles, and that this physical condition is known for its effect on the mental state.

After a year, the proportions of my body have become more balanced. People notice the change, and marvel; how slim you've gotten!! (Actually, I still weigh the same).

Eight days of menstruation have come down to 3–5 days.

The need to smoke decreased. I cut down from 15–20 cigarettes a day to 2–7 a day, until I stopped altogether. It took no effort at all. I just don't feel like it.

I also feel that my body's resistance has increased — wounds, etc., heal much more easily.

A pleasant surprise was that my moustache came off! My

upper lip is now quite hairless — without cosmetic help. A few hairs that were growing on my chin have also gone away. According to Paula, there's nothing surprising about it. It happens when muscles in these spots start working.

As for the pressure on the back of my neck — it hasn't bothered me for three months now. The problem, in a less severe form, has 'dropped' to the left shoulder, where there is still some strain and discomfort. Now I also feel one of the vertebra in my back reacting to the strain in my left shoulder. But there are daily changes and progress in everything.

There have been difficulties on the road to recovery. Exercising so much and so stubbornly demanded a lot of will-power and patience, especially at first. But Paula was very patient with me (more than I was with myself), and made it clear to me there are ups and downs along the way.

Paula conveyed to me faith in my body — faith that it wants to, and can, mend itself. It progresses at its own pace, and cannot be rushed. This belief, that one shouldn't push, that things come in their own time, has also brought me a new tranquility and self-confidence.

Yoram — Dyslexia

(Parents' testimonial)

Yoram was referred to Paula Garbourg for treatment at the age of 11, when he was in the fourth or fifth grade. He had trouble reading fluently, didn't understand numbers, had difficulty in comprehending the essential concept of a number, and was therefore, of course, unable to participate fully in the arithmetic lessons at school.

At the same time he was prone to be restless, both at school and at home, which manifested itself in the inability to sit in one place, and a need to leave the classroom from time to time and to run.

He was also prone to falling down, chiefly on his head. It seemed as though everywhere Yoram went, his head would go before him and fall on something, or something would fall on it. As a result he had several concussions, and had to have stitches in his head 4–5 times.

From the time he was a small child it was clear that he had an excellent intelligence and was extremely alert and restless. He was then diagnosed as hyperactive.

He was popular in kindergarten, excelling in social sport and anything that entailed a lot of movement, such as running, etc. In contrast, he adamantly refused to take part in all the activities — such as drawing, constructing shapes, etc. — that demanded hand-eye coordination. In psychological tests administered at the age of five and a half to determine whether he was ready for school, a gap was found between general intellectual capacity and performance where perception of forms or grasp of abstractions was involved. It was not clear then whether it was a matter of general developmental lag or a specific deficiency.

In the second grade, with the aid of a special reading and arithmetic teacher, he got to the point where he knew the technique of reading, but read slowly and with great difficulty. His handwriting was terrible, notably for its lack of clarity and for switched letters. His teachers characterized him as a typical dyslectic child.

In the third grade he barely coped with concepts of ten and twenty, and was unable to perform any abstract operation verbally.

At the same time he was ambitious and made an effort to progress. After half an hour or an hour of exertion, he could burst out crying at his inability to go on.

Five or six years have passed since he met Paula.

Yoram worked intensively with Paula at the start, and later with one of her pupils for an hour a week. After a short time, about a month or two, a great change was already evident in the boy, especially in his studies. He began to understand more. His tremendous difficulty with abstract thinking and concentration was gradually disappearing. We saw the child starting to come to grips with theoretical material and even mastering it. The process of overcoming intellectual difficulties is, in my opinion, going on until this day, and each time there is a further advance in this respect.

Today he is in the ninth grade in high school, and is an average student in most subjects. During his school years he had major difficulties twice (besides reading and arithmetic at the beginning), and they were in the study of foreign languages. Every time he had to learn a new set of letters — once Arabic and once English — his difficulties in reading comprehension came back. But now he overcomes these difficulties with minimal help and much more easily than before. He has stopped falling on his head, though he engages in several kinds of sport, including sports that especially require a sense of balance, such as riding horseback and surfing.

We have viewed Paula's work, and later the work of her assistant, as an on-going process that accompanies Yoram's growing up. There is no doubt that it has been a crucial factor in the boy's ability to remain in the school framework and to discover more and more of his inherent possibilities, that had been unable to find expression.

And so, after five years, we are still being confronted with surprises in the development of the boy's thinking — especially in contrast with the tremendous difficulties he had to start with. This is currently manifesting itself in the fact that he is coping very respectably with high school mathematics and physics.

In our estimation, Yoram's opportunity to avail himself of Paula's beneficial method is vital for him today, too, and certainly will be in the coming years of intellectual and physical development — perhaps until the end of his adolescence. But we can't predict that in advance. We watch the boy's development with satisfaction and delight, and are grateful to Paula and her pupil, Yoli Magnat.

Haggai — Hyperactivity

(Psychologist's testimonial)
Haggai aged 7, was sent to Paula by a psychologist , the director of the Psychological Service in one of Israel's centrally located cities. When he reached Paula, he was in the first grade. It was impossible to teach with him in the classroom; every five minutes he would go out to the toilet. His face would contort when he refused to do something he was asked to do. His fingers were clenched all the time.

When an attack got worse, he would thrash about like a fish — his whole body, would stiffen as he lashed out in all directions with his hands and feet, kicking and punching anyone who tried to restrain him. Whenever he was seized by such an attack he would run wildly from one corner of the room to another. He seemed to be incapable of controlling himself.

At the beginning his mother had to be present during treatment and sit beside him. After a few sessions it was possible to let the mother go. Haggai gradually started to calm down, to listen to instructions and to carry them out.

Today Haggai is an ordinary pupil, sitting in class throughout the required hours of study. The contortions and spasms have gone away, and if he feels discomfort he knows what to do to overcome it. He is a good student and in some subjects a very good one — where previously he had needed supplementary tutoring in everything. The improvement in his physical state has caused improvement in his emotional state and behavior, and a steep rise in his school achievement. His mother says the teacher put it this way: "If I hadn't seen with my own eyes the change and progress that took place in this child within the space of three short months, I would have said it was a fabrication."

Ali — Hyperactivity

(Psychologist's testimonial)
Ali is a five-and-a-half-year-old boy who was examined by psychologists and diagnosed as a hyperactive child with a low frustration threshold and lack of concentration.

His behavior at home was difficult. Whenever he was dissatisfied he would shout and fling himself on the floor. In kindergarten he behaved very aggressively. His mother and the psychologist feared that his behavior would prevent him from fitting into a normal school framework. That is how he came to the Institute for treatment.

Following treatment, his behavior at home improved. He stopped flinging himself on the floor, and became calmer.

Today he is a first-grade pupil who fits into his class very well. When his teacher was asked about his integration in the class, she said she didn't see anything unusual in his behavior, and that he is an ordinary pupil.

Gidi — Asthma

(Medical report and own letter)
Gidi, 17 years old, Israeli born, student.
Referred by treating physician because of asthma. Despite protracted treatment with medication, no improvement in his condition.

Medical history:
1) At 7 months — spastic bronchitis.
2) From age 7 suffered from asthma, shortness of breath, coughs and colds. Treated with anti-asthmatic medications including inhalations, with no improvement.
3) Backaches.
4) Stomach aches and constipation.
5) Toothaches.
6) Dizziness and fatigue.
7) Dryness of eyes.
8) Sensation of cold in hands and feet.
9) Complaints of downcast moods.

At intake:
Stooped young man, general physical condition normal, depressive mood.
Treatment:
Sphincter muscle exercises were performed, partly under supervision and partly in independent work. His condition improved. Improvement started shortly after treatment began; and after fifteen months all complaints disappeared. Today, two years after the first session, the young man is serving in the IDF

without any problems.

Gidi writes:

To Paula with esteem:

I wanted to thank you in a few words for all you've done for me, and what you're doing every day for a lot of other people who have had the privilege to meet you and receive treatment from you.

About your healing method, I don't think there's any doubt that it works since its effect has already been proved on a lot of people, and it has helped with many medical problems that wouldn't seem to be connected with each other. The exercises worked wonderfully for me, too, and I'm glad I had the chance to undergo this treatment.

At first the exercises seem illogical and completely unconnected, but little by little in the course of exercising you begin to understand and to realize that the exercises are connected and do complement one another. By doing the exercises, you begin to understand the workings of the sophisticated machine called the human body. You see that the feet aren't separate, and the mouth isn't separate, or for example, that the back is connected with the action of the nose and they work together, so that if one member of the body is not functioning as it should the whole system is immediately disrupted, which makes itself felt in symptoms elsewhere in the body. On the other hand, if the whole system is operating properly, and all its 'parts' are working, the body's harmony is felt immediately. You feel you are walking differently, eating differently, breathing differently, and in general feeling different. Because just as the organs are connected with one another, so, too, is the emotional feeling connected with the body's state of health. They are, in fact, two sides of the same coin, improving in parallel.

Dalia — Incontinence

I came to Paula following an operation for a prolapsed bladder. I was very miserable because half a year after the operation, the aggravating symptoms of lack of bladder control had come back.

The situation was intolerable, particularly during trips and in places where there was no toilet nearby.

I began to work intensively with Paula five sessions a week, as well as working on my own at home. My condition gradually began to improve, and after a few months I was able to control my bladder. Already after the first session I removed the corset I was wearing under doctor's orders.

Paula's exercises radiate to all parts of the body, so that many other problems I had were solved in the course of the work.

I had serious problems with the back of my neck, being unable to move my head freely. So I had been receiving orthopedic treatment for about 20 years, including massage, stretching exercises, short waves and sedatives. I had almost given up hope, and decided to come to terms with the disability.

Another problem I had had since early childhood was constipation. Thinking it an irremediable inborn defect, I had never done anything about it. I also suffered from severe pains when menstruating. I must stress that I came to Paula because of my bladder problem, and the rest of the problems were solved in the course of the work.

Paula's exercises are also soothing during attacks of headache and depression.

Paula taught me that it is possible to live differently and be freed from a great many aches and pains.

Of course the method isn't magical. You have to work hard and stick to it. There are exercises that can be done while working, watching TV, or traveling. You have to know which exercise to do in various situations: like lifting something heavy, or going up stairs. It's a way of life that becomes routine. Of course if you neglect working on the exercises for a while, the undesirable symptoms start coming back.

The exercising yielded surprising results. It brought me back to normal life and enabled me to do hard physical work again. On our kibbutz, I work in the kitchen.

I don't have enough words of thanks and appreciation for Paula.

Carmela — Bed-wetting

(Mother's testimonial)
Carmela was already eight years old and still wetting her bed every night. We had already been told dozens of ways to break a child of bed-wetting. We had tried most of them but nothing helped. For a long time we used to wake her up in the middle of the night and take her to the bathroom. It helped sometimes, for that same night, but on nights when we didn't do it, the bed-wetting came back. We tried not letting her drink from early afternoon. We tried having her launder the wet sheets herself. Nothing helped. Every morning the child would get up wet and dejected, and all of us would be dejected and annoyed together with her.

In total despair we went to a child psychologist to ask her help. There was already no doubt in our minds that the problem was emotional.

The psychologist talked with us and the child, and decided it would be worthwhile for us to try meeting Paula Garbourg to see whether she might be able to help Carmela. We started going to Paula. The treatment went on for several months and was difficult and exhausting for all of us. The child was obliged to give up a great part of her daily pursuits to work on the exercises and we tried to be with her while she exercised, to keep her from feeling so wretched. At first we were discouraged. The exercising was hard and a bother and we didn't see any progress. And then, suddenly, one morning the child got up dry. We thought it was a fluke. It was hard to believe. But the dry mornings got increasingly frequent, and our hopes grew with them. Occasionally there were relapses, and it was again hard to believe we were making progress. There were moments when we despaired and wanted to stop, but we knew we had nothing to lose and kept on with it.

And then the child stopped wetting. We started seeing improvement in her posture, progress in her gym lessons at school, and there was a feeling that her whole muscle system was getting stronger. We were overjoyed at the realization that we were at the end of the road. The child still kept exercising daily for a long time, until the happy moment arrived at long last. The treatment was over.

It's hard to describe how happy we are and how grateful to Paula for extricating us from this problem that had seemed to us to be insoluble. She gave our daughter help for which we will always thank her. Almost 4 years have passed since the treatment. Carmela is now 12 years old, and there hasn't been a single recurrence of bed-wetting.

Dita — Insomnia and Other Disturbances

About six years ago I was referred to Mrs. Paula Garbourg by a graphologist. My chief problem has expressed itself in chronic sleeplessness over a period of many years, which brought increasing use of sleeping pills in its wake. Not only was my dependence on the pills absolute, but it was rising steadily. Talks with a psychologist over a period of three years brought some improvement in the situation, and she referred me to a psychiatrist so that he could try to overcome the problem with medications. The outcome of this transfer was addition of three kinds of medication. At the high point of the treatment I was consuming eight pills a day including, of course, the sleeping pills as well.

I should mention here that besides my insomnia, I was in a state of total inability to become emotionally attached to other people — including even my own children — and I always bore with me a bundle of 'minor' ills that included excessive perspiration, radically irregular digestion, acne pimples that refused to go away despite having been treated in all the customary ways, incessant pains at the back of my neck, and rather frequent headaches.

Despite all this, my outer image was that of a highly successful and active person — perfectly 'normal'.

I reached Mrs. Garbourg in a state of complete lack of confidence and almost total unwillingness, with the distinct intention of utilizing her assistance only for a brief trial period — while continuing my psychiatric treatment.

I can't even start to explain how lucky I was to get to know Paula Garbourg's method. If during the time just before I went to her I was asking myself every evening. 'Will I have the strength to suffer my life one more day?" my distinct feeling after the day I first exercised with her was 'I'll hold out till next time'. I didn't demand more. The lessons were conducted without any touching and almost without words. Dry instructions were given to carry out certain physical actions. After a month I was able to call the graphologist (at his request) and report 'I think it's helping'.

Two weeks after the first lesson I stopped taking all medications except for half a sleeping pill. In the third week I stopped the talks with the psychiatrist, despite his vigorous protests. I fought hard for another year against the last survivor of the medications — in the form of 1/2 – 1/3 tablet — until I won. It's only with an effort that I can now succeed in reconstructing those nightmare hours before falling asleep. After about a month I began getting compliments on my youthful appearance. After about two months my acne disappeared for good. All the disagreeable symptoms that had been my constant uninvited companions in previous years went away and didn't come back. My physical fitness increased greatly, and so did my ability to perform tasks that had been hard for me many years earlier. My emotional stability changed beyond all recognition, as did my attitude towards people and things.

To sum up:
Although the time I underwent treatment is long past, and despite the fact that I have on occasion been required to meet demands for emotional and physical efforts far greater than those demanded of me before — there is within me a support on which I can rely at any time, and so — I feel good.

Tsipora — Manic Depression

In 1969 I spent a month in the Shalvata mental hospital with a diagnosis of manic depression. I was given Lithium tablets there. (Since getting out of there I don't use any pills, and I didn't resort to pills of any kind before that, either, except to bring a temperature down).

I got to Shalvata after five hard years of marriage, having a two-year-old son. All those years I had lived in anxiety and insecurity, with a feeling that I wasn't worth anything and I was a nincompoop.

I didn't cry during the years of my marriage. I hadn't perspired several years before getting married. My periods lasted seven days. I had fungus on my toenails. I had a tendency to eczema on the soles of my feet since my army induction at the age of 18.

Already in the first lesson, what made me want to stay on with Paula was the feeling of warmth that started in the middle of my abdomen above the navel and spread all over my body enveloping me without talk or explanation. Suddenly I sensed that what I was looking for in life was in me, inside me; the pleasant warmth was coming to me from inside myself. Suddenly I felt a sort of inner preparedness, as though I were flying for a second. I remember that when I went out from the lesson and walked in the street it was the first time in a long time that I wasn't afraid of people looking at me. I didn't feel they 'knew' I was a nincompoop. They just looked and went about their business.

I kept going to Paula once a week.

The second time I remember as a leap forward came after

about two years' work with Paula. One day I burst out crying in mid-lesson. I was almost scared of myself, and I covered my face with my hands. I'd forgotten tears existed. I always felt anguish but the tears didn't come, and all of a sudden — my eyes were wet! It was a 'far-out' feeling, really beautiful, and since then things have started moving little by little in all areas. Today, the tears always come to me at the right time and place. I sweat. The fungus has vanished from my toenails. My periods are only 3 days long. The outbursts of anger I used to have are much fewer. And what is most important, today I live with the feeling that I am worth something in my own eyes, and that is a wonderful feeling, which gives me peace of mind and inner security and good contact with people.

Uri — Autism

A. The psychologist's account:
The following report was given us by a child psychologist who evaluated drawings done by Uri when he was coming to the clinic for treatment.

Drawings by Uri, a 13-year-old autistic boy, were collected over a period of about six weeks — from March 4 to April 22, 1979. Development is evident in his manner of drawing, and changes in the character of the drawings.

Drawing 1: Blobs of color dabbed on without any order are salient, and it is apparent that they were made with a great deal of aggressiveness. The drawing was done with much force, and in an attempt to use a pen the sheet on which the drawing was made was torn.

Drawing 2: The aggressive element is still salient. an intention to draw round shapes and fill them in with color is evident here, but the filling overflows the frame drastically, and is still done with much force. It is worth mentioning that the choice of colors in these drawings is especially conspicuous for its gloominess. The boy chose dark, gloomy colors, and this may be explained by the gloomy mood he was in. Therefore, also the anger that made him invest so much energy in his drawings.

Drawing 3: Serious progress is apparent. The boy has switched from gloomy colors to more cheerful ones. The circular shapes still exist, but the circles are open now. The color is spread with less pressure, and an attempt is evident to create varied forms like a green leaf and a face.

Drawing 4: Color may be disregarded, since he did not have colors. The overall form, too, has regressed towards disorganized doodling. The same applies to Drawing 5, which in my opinion is inferior to Drawing 3.

Drawing 6: Here the boy obviously tried to draw structured and controlled shapes, broke free from the need to fill the page, and his earlier circular shapes (circle inside circle) became circle alongside circle. The circles have also become more clearcut in form, so as to express his intentions — for example, an attempt to draw a man.

Drawing 7: An attempt to draw a face is apparent. Here, too, aggressiveness is manifest in the pressure of pen and color on the paper, but the drawing is structured and deliberate and shows some method.

Drawing 8: Even greater progress is expressed. Here an attempt is made to draw some sort of creature. The face and body are apparent, though the pressure of the writing implement is still greater than in Drawings 3 and 6. Another doodle, drawn on the back of Drawing 7, should be mentioned: this drawing exhibits distinct intention, and a breaking free from the incessant circles.

Drawing 9 and 10: There is a serious regression, a return to smudges of color that are unstructured and aggressive, although not as much so as the first drawings.

To sum up, development may beyond any doubt be said to be in evidence here. According to the therapist, the regression in the last two drawings reflects the child's disappointment and anger after having been told that the treatment he loved so much was coming to an end.

B. The Institute therapist's account:

Condition at intake: At first, upon coming into the Institute he would walk around, touching the walls and banging his head against them. He used to crawl under a bed. His parents testified that at home, too, he banged his head on the wall a great deal and also hid. He had frequent fits of rage and crying.

Speech: He would 'get stuck' on a word from a sentence he had heard and repeat it endlessly. The word 'I' did not exist in his lexicon. He did not speak in the first person, but only repeated what others said to him, without changing the form.

Drawing: He drew one permanent drawing — a single circle, or a circle within a circle, colored inside with a lot of pressure.

The treatment: I started with massaging his forehead — I gave the massage at the spot he banged his head on the principle that what the body wants is what it needs. The massage would calm him down. He'd ask for more, taking my hand and putting it on his forehead. He even asked his parents to give him this kind of massage. Later on, he asked verbally as well for 'massages'.

After a number of sessions he stopped touching the walls, and after his head was massaged stopped banging it against the wall. He also stopped crawling under the bed.

Speech: He repeats words less and the change is great — he has started answering sentences. He cooperates until a dialogue has been created.

Drawing: He has drawn a human figure and even said it was a 'man'.

Gail — Retardation

(Sister's testimonial)
Born November, 9, 1955. Not toilet trained until age five or six. Slow, unintelligible speech at first, later learned to speak better, but retained a definite speech impediment. Extreme myopia, not recognized until age 6, when doctor at hospital diagnosed her as retarded. Mother did not believe this. She thought that difficulty in speech, terrible eyesight, and extremely strained home environment accounted for much of Gail's behavioral dysfunction. The doctor had said that she had minimal brain damage, but that the brain damage was not great enough to account for her behavioral problems, which were hyperactivity and inability to function in a social climate of her age group, and that she was aggressive physically when frustrated by the fact that she could not make herself understood by others due to her speech impediment.

She went to various schools (normal class), and eventually was thrown out of each one because she could not pay attention and was disrupting the class with her hyperactive behavior. She began to take a liquid tranquilizer which calmed her down considerably, but also dulled her senses. Mother finally put her in a school for retarded children out of lack of choice, for the time being, until she could manage to find her other forms of help.

Mother finally took her out of that school because she was regressing in her behavior to the point of imitating all the idiosyncratic abberations in behavior of all the other children, plus she was not learning anything academically. So my mother and I taught her to read and write at home. When things were explained to her in a reasonably explicit manner, with patience, she had no problem learning.

So most of her years from 8 to 14 were spent at home, all the while my mother trying to find her help from any reasonable source.

At age 13, Gail went to Dr. A.J. Kirshner, who gave her motor-visual training in his clinic and thus rid her of her hyperactive behavior and the tranquilizers.

She started to wear a contact lens in her right eye. Her left eye was what is called a lazy eye and did not work very well with the other eye. But the contact lens did not fit very well (unknown to us at the time) and gave her a lot of trouble, like infections and soreness. Her behavior was much improved from the six months of work with Dr. Kirshner, but she still had temper tantrums when she was frustrated.

She went to a special class at the high school until she was 16, but it was mainly a baby-sitting service.

She had seen various doctors, psychologists and social workers during her childhood and teenage years, and none could agree on her diagnosis. Some said she was emotionally disturbed, others said she was a slow learner, and still a few said she was retarded. But despite all her difficulties — poor eye-hand coordination, extremely bad eyesight, very sloppy, swaying walk, poor speech, slow activity and inability to do things (chores around the house) quickly, no friends to relate to, etc. — she could still take care of a house on her own though slowly, cook simple meals, take care of her personal needs, read slowly, write, do arithmetic, and travel around the city on her own.

At age 20 or 21, she went to Israel to be in Dr. Feuerstein's program at Hadassah-WIZO for young adults and high-school-age children with so called learning problems. Gail was there for 2 years and improved a lot socially, but still walked very awkwardly and had a great deal of trouble expressing herself emotionally through her speech, and was still extremely slow at doing chores around the house, reading, etc.

She started Paula's program and within a very short time (about two weeks) I could already see improvements taking place in her. She became generally more coordinated, she began to walk much, much straighter, and not sway from side to side, her left eye, which had always been crossed, began to straighten; but the most amazing change of all, in my opinion, was that she became much more able to express herself in speech, and to express exactly how she felt at the time, without difficulty, as she had never been able to before. And, perhaps as a result, she calmed down considerably emotionally.

Her eye-hand coordination also became much, much better and she learned to sweep a floor with ease, which had been an overwhelmingly difficult task for her before. She became much quicker in her general movements and in doing her chores in general. Her whole face seemed to take on a completely different look; she seemed to glow, she had color in her cheeks, and for the first time in her life, her face took on an interested, bright, alert, almost cheerful expression, instead of her usual deadpan look. Her bowels started to move regularly, which was quite amazing in itself, because she had, since birth, always been plagued by constipation, and now she was going to the bathroom once or twice, or sometimes even 3 times daily, since she started the exercises.

Gail unfortunately had to return to Canada after 2 or 3 months with Paula; but even in that short time she made great strides in becoming more 'normalized' physically and emotionally. If she improved so much in such a short time, who knows how far she could have gone, if she had been able to continue Paula's treatment for, let's say, a year? The odds certainly seem in favor of her improvement.

Amiran — Retardation

(Psychologist's account)
Twenty-nine-year-old Amiram, diagnosed as retarded, was referred to me by the director of the psychological service in a centrally located city in Israel.

His outward appearance was unusual, attracting people's attention in the street. His body was conspicuously lacking in proportion, with an elongated, narrow head, a blank stare and a pale, frozen expressionless face. His posture was sloppy — head and neck thrust forward, back rounded, and arms dangling listlessly in front of his body.

He walked with a wide straddle, uncertainly, often stumbling and even falling for lack of balance. He spoke loudly, sometimes actually shouting. His speech was very hard to understand, and monotonous.

Amiram tried to work at gardening but things would fall out of his hands, flowerpots would break and the wheelbarrow would overturn. He also fell down frequently. His general mood was negative and defeatist.

After nine months of treatment, four times a week to start with and then less often. Amiram's appearance changed. He doesn't attract attention, walks confidently erect, his sense of balance has improved, and he doesn't fall down. His body proportions have changed and his face has filled out. His hands do not hang down like unwanted appendages, but function properly. His pallor has vanished, and so has his blank stare. He is now working as an office boy and is earning money. (His mother used to pay people to consent to employ him in various places). He doesn't shout, and his speech is pleasant and distinct.

He is studying English and learning to play the recorder. His mother says he is progressing nicely.

When his physical condition improved, so did his mood and his emotional, mental and overall condition, and he succeeded in getting regular employment.

Malka — Asymmetry

For years I had been used to seeing in the mirror that my left eye was higher and lighter in color than my right.

I knew that every dressmaker had to be warned about my dropping left shoulder, because if I didn't call her attention to it the garment would come out crooked. My left breast drooped lower than the right.

I never liked my left shoe. No matter what kind of shoes they were, the left was always more creased and ugly than the right.

Buying shoes was an exhausting chore, because it's devilishly hard to find a matching pair of shoes to fit a left foot that's almost a whole size larger than the right — with a left leg that has been asleep for 17 years...

I got used to all these 'trifles'. After all, who is exempt from them?

There remained only one problem: the pains in my back and in my left leg, which were very hard to overlook. Any work or activity that involved standing for more than ten minutes aroused my fears.

But when I reached a state where I couldn't sleep and I spent night after night in pain and frustration — I went to see Noah, Paula Garbourg's pupil.

We arranged to start treatment in the summer of 1978. I waited curiously to start this 'odd' kind of gymnastics. My journey with Noah proved fascinating. At every session I learned to recognize that I have a body, and that it has functions I wasn't acquainted with. Strange — it was my body, and was yet so unfamiliar. I learned to pay attention to small details. We met twice a week. On the other days I worked a little by myself. And actually, maybe I learned from Noah to like my body. It seems I did. Suddenly everything was important. Things I hadn't noticed for years became meaningful.

I remember that summer of 1978 fondly, for those were the most intense months I ever had. I slept only about four or five hours a night, and was more awake than I had ever been in my life. I studied long hours and my receptivity was high.

Since then, I exercise on my own almost every morning.My backaches have disappeared, and with them my fear of prolonged standing.

A few months ago I suddenly felt signs of life in the numb muscle of my left leg, and almost complete sensation has now returned in that muscle. I've also noticed that my eyes are level with each other. I think even my shoulder droops less.

My walk has changed very much. I don't run with the upper part of my trunk bent down. That is, I've stopped 'galloping'. My left breast has 'climbed' to where it belongs.

There is hardly any difference between my left shoe and my right — the two wear out very similarly. And in shopping for shoes, the problem of an unusually long left foot has disappeared.

In trying to sum up, it seems to me I have simply become younger and healthier.

Nechama — Ageing

My acquaintance with Paula Garbourg started some 25 years ago, when in the context of my work I was looking for additional ways to activate the tongue (I was then engaged in correcting speech defects). Paula refused to teach me her method or explain it to me, but said she was prepared to work with me since I had 'problems' — which, according to her, were written all over my face. Needless to say, her remarks made a very strange impression, to say the least. But that is beside the point, I was at that time right after quite a severe illness and in a very rundown general condition, in fact at the beginning of a clear-cut typical ageing process. My legs were getting thin, the muscles of my inner thighs were dwindling, my toes had become weak and were 'riding' on the big toes, I was beginning to get the bandy legs so typical of old women. My knees, which also hurt a great deal, had become so weak that I sometimes had trouble controlling them, especially when standing. The wrinkles on my face were proliferating and getting deeper, the skin was dry, and the whole eye region was strewn with blackheads that provided a lot of work for the cosmetician. Serious changes were found in the upper and lower vertebrae of my spine, and just before my visit to Paula I had ordered — at the doctor's orders — a corset. (As customary at that time, it was a thick, stiff, heavy corset for the back and pelvis. Once I decided to work with Paula, I canceled the order.) Pains in the back of the neck, the shoulders, the hips, and most of all in the knees, which had been my daily fare for many years, had increased to the point of terrible torment. Besides all that, I was already then on a strict diet for gastritis and colitis, and also had hemorrhoids in an advanced stage.

Nevertheless, despite everything, I took offence at Paula's offer and replied that I didn't understand what she had to do with a healthy woman like me!

I am citing this seemingly incidental fact primarily because it is so typical of many people who are ashamed to be considered sick, who ignore their suffering and their pains and refuse to look after themselves, focusing all their attention on their objectives and activities in a desperate effort to 'overcome', to hold out and stay away from any kind of clinic — when at least partial relief for their ailments is within reach. In the first years after I became acquainted with Paula's method, this thought used to bother me constantly. Every day I would want to approach some complete stranger in the street and give them Paula's address.

Besides that, I want to stress the chronic nature and advanced stage of my 'problems'. These ills, or at least part of them, were 'old-timers' and the damage they had inflicted on my spine and digestive system had become an inalterable fact. But I still divide the years of my life, starting from about the age of 35, into two periods — before and after Paula. I think one of the things that made it possible for me to accept from Paula what she had to offer was her awareness of my condition, which kept her from entertaining any illusions. It was clear to me that I had come to her not to replace wrecked limbs, but to prevent, as far as possible, their further ruin, to arrest the process of ageing, and to learn how to live more correctly.

I did quite thorough work with Paula for one year. My

body's 'awakening' was rather slow, its response stretching out over most of that year, stage by stage. Things were 'happening', and from time to time I would understand anew why Paula is not willing to explain her work; and that only someone who has worked at it thoroughly enough and long enough is capable of understanding it.

Most of the things that happened to me that year were very obvious. My toes straightened. My feet, which had always — even when I was young — been very slender and thin, put on 'padding'. My calf and thigh muscles rehabilitated and returned to their previous shape. The skin of my legs regained its former sheen. The tendency of bandy legs went away for good. My face filled out and most of the wrinkles smoothed out or at least became less deep. The blackheads vanished without a trace — until this very day. The same happened with the hemorrhoids, and my bowel movements have improved greatly.

All these changes were concrete and visible. I went to see the doctor who had treated me when I was ill. When she saw me on the examination couch she gave an astonished cry and blurted out: 'What's happened to you? Why, you look twenty years younger!" But when she realized the nature of the explanation, she interrupted me sharply and wasn't willing to hear it.

But the invisible transformations, which only I can sense and appreciate properly, were far more meaningful. I used to recall myself as I was when I first came to Paula, as another woman. If I wished to put it in a single sentence, I might say I had started to sense the ground under my feet, to sense myself as being of one piece, and to use my body as such in my everyday life. I had learned to consume less energy, and to release myself from the tensions that accumulated in me following physical and emotional exertion. I had generally become much more flexible than ever before, even when I was young, and capable of coping with harder physical tasks.

At the end of the year I stopped my sessions with Paula and went on working on my own.

Till this day, I haven't stopped working on myself, and new things keep happening to me all the time, mostly not of the concrete and visible variety, among them some that I can't prove actually happened — but am still convinced they did. In so long a lifetime and at such an advanced age, the 'amortization' makes its advances, too, and I haven't the shadow of a doubt that its mark on my body would be immeasurably greater were it not for Paula's work, which I have kept up — though not always as often and as much as I should. Several times during these years I have 'attacked' various aches and pains, some new and some 'reincarnated' — and in most cases I was their match, at least partially, sometimes with Paula's advice or assistance.

I cannot conclude my personal story without mentioning two things that happened to me, and I think I won't be exaggerating if I term them dramatic.

The first happened at the end of the first year after I stopped working with Paula. As I said, I kept working daily during that year. Several days before the 'event', I was standing and talking with a friend. The conversation flowed and developed into an argument, and suddenly I felt — I even said so to my friend — a distinct change taking place in my breathing while talking, both in the way I was taking in air between sentences and in the way I was letting it out during a sentence. The change was not only distinct but sudden. I must mention here that while Paula does accompany most of her exercises with breathing (for accuracy's sake, with exhalations), she definitely does not teach breathing — at any rate she never taught me. So this change in me took place entirely unconsciously and unexpectedly, as a result of two years' work.

Several days later I participated in an outing that included several hours of continuous walking. I've been a walker all my life so there was nothing new to me in walking per se. But something strange happened to the way I walked, and I told my companions I was walking differently from ever before. I even explained that I was walking with the inside muscles of my legs, I had in the past heard about the principle of 'walking in' more than once from gym teachers at school. But I had never succeeded in doing it then, beyond a few steps consciously taken, without any effect on my day-to-day walking.

On the day of the outing there was a severe *khamsin* (a hot, dry east wind) and the walking, which lasted several hours, exerted my leg muscles very intensively. When I got home I took a shower and lay down to rest. A few minutes later I felt a sort of strange streaming all over my legs, something like thousands of tiny ants running. It lasted a minute at the most. When, a bit frightened, I turned on the light, the white sheet under and alongside my legs was covered with hairs! The legs themselves were almost completely hairless.

Since then, my legs are no hairier than those of most of the women I know.

A person to whom Paula's technique is foreign will certainly not understand why I have connected these two changes, in breathing and in walking (not to speak of the hair shedding). For Paula's pupils the connection is very obvious, especially since the two things happened to me at the same time, with no conscious direction or intervention, genuinely of their own accord. The explanation, then, is that during two years of working with Paula's method, the sphincter-muscle system had organized itself. As for the hair shedding — on that first morning I described earlier Paula told me, among other things, that my legs were so hairy because I was walking wrong!

Leah — Sterility

During my first year of marriage I took precautions not to become pregnant.

During the second year we had intercourse freely for ten months with the intention of my getting pregnant. I then had my uterus X-rayed, which showed everything to be all right — clear passages and good dispersion.

After that, I started taking my temperature every morning to see if I was ovulating. According to the temperature chart my ovulation was irregular. I started getting Chlomophide (Ikalomine) therapy and the ovulation straightened itself out. After a few treatments. Cinorel pills were added. All the signs showed normal ovulation, but without a pregnancy. This treatment went on for about a year and a half or two with a few months of interruption. The results of a periscopic examination showed everything normal.

On the fifth year of our marriage I started on Pergonal treatment. After three periods of treatment I decided to stop it, because of the risk involved in taking this drug that had yielded no results.

During my sixth year of marriage, I didn't receive any treatment, and though we had intercourse freely I still didn't get pregnant. At the end of that year, at the age of 28, I started exercising with Paula Garbourg on the recommendation of the psychologist who treated me during these years.

I started exercising daily for two weeks at Paula's institute, and to do exercises at home. I did the exercises mechanically at first, and in a short time I felt how the muscles of my face and mouth, for example, were relaxing, and the muscles of the anus and vulva were beginning to work harmoniously with those of the mouth and eyes. In time, I felt freer and more relaxed and my general feeling improved. I also started wearing flat shoes without heels, and discovered they made walking easier and stabilized the body. During all this time, whenever I felt tension building up in my body I would do a few exercises and my body would be released from the tension. After the first two weeks, I kept going to the Institute twice a week and doing daily exercises at home.

It's worth mentioning that the change was evident both in my outward appearance and in my mood.

Half a year from the day I started exercising, I got pregnant with no medical treatment at all. The pregnancy was a natural and healthy one from the start, and progressed normally.

In the sixth month I went back to the Institute to prepare for childbirth, under the guidance of Paula and her pupil Noah. I did easy exercises that do not require strength, and exercises that enable the body to work on its own.

Throughout the months of advanced pregnancy, although my belly was relatively large for my body, I felt no special burden.

It should be mentioned that all through the pregnancy, the doctor's examinations showed my cervix to be very flexible, and all signs showed that a natural birth was to be expected.

At the end of the ninth month, on the expected day, I was admitted for childbirth because the water had broken without labor pains or other indications. After preparation for delivery I was hooked up to a monitor which showed that, although I was feeling no pain, there were regular labor spasms enabling the delivery to progress. This painless labor went on for about five hours, and I then gave birth to a 4.150 kg. daughter in a natural delivery.

It's worth mentioning that my daughter came out of the womb and started crying at once, with no assistance from the doctor.

Robert — Impotence

(Therapist's account)
Robert was referred to me by a graphologist. His main problem was impotence, owing to which he avoided attachments with women. Outwardly, Robert was 'a man', his shoulders very broad and inclined forward, his arms rolled in a way that inclined his hands slightly backwards and bent his elbows. His standing posture was spraddle-legged. There were deep inward curvatures at the nape of the neck and the waist. His eyes protruded slightly more than usual (he was short-sighted). He also suffered from shortness of breath, resulting partly from massive smoking and a need to urinate frequently even at night, as well as excessive excretion of the sweat glands, particularly in the palms of the hands and the soles of the feet.

I should add that he came to me following psychiatric treatment and working out with a certain kind of gymnastics method, neither of which had helped.

While the 'classic' process of improvement is almost always built on forward leaps and backslidings, Robert's progress was slow but constant. At one and the same time with feeling better physically in general, he overcame his principal problem. About a year later he married and fathered his first son.

The change in the way he stood and walked was apparent: his feet were closer together and his shoulders had 'moved' backward, so that he seemed to have grown taller; his short-windedness had improved considerably and he smoked less. His night's sleep was undisturbed, the excessive perspiration had stopped, and the look on his face was no longer frozen. Robert's case may be said to have been one of success without undue shocks or drastic changes in his living habits, and was particularly convincing to me as a teacher. For Robert may be defined as a realistic type, who was not religiously carried away by the method but did the exercises with a perseverance that brought him the result he was waiting for — and perhaps even more.

Amnon — Problems of a Conductor

My vocation, that of an orchestra conductor, involves physical work and emotional and mental stress. It is a fact that most conductors have back, shoulder, or neck trouble. I, too, had almost constant tension in the shoulders, and sometimes I also got backaches.

I came to Paula when I was already about 54 years old. After only a few sessions I already felt relief in the shoulders. I had a sense of release and lightness after every session. After several months I interrupted treatment for half a year to travel abroad, and had no trouble. I came back anyway for weekly lessons, and only then did the real progress start. I reached a state where I could stand and conduct for hours on end at difficult rehearsals and concerts without any muscle strain whatsoever. People who had known me for years told me my appearance had changed for the better, primarily in a sense of freedom and release that directly affected the members of the orchestra as well. My own feeling is that I have grown a bit taller and my neck has lengthened.

Many of my performances entail traveling, with me at the wheel. This always used to be one of the main causes of my neck trouble. I started doing various exercises while driving, and this problem went away, too.

Amalia — Improved Appearance

I came to Mrs Paula Garbourg for treatment when I was about 24 years old, lacking in body consciousness, fat, suffering from pains in my left arm which had been fractured when I was a girl, and finding it hard to breathe when climbing to high places. Working on my body for about two years with Paula I gradually succeeded in reducing by about 20 kilograms. I began to understand and feel my body, and to acquire physical self-criticism.

The pains in my left arm during changes in the weather have disappeared almost entirely, and my capacity for physical exertion has improved greatly, especially on excursions.

I have learned to employ my body to my own ends, and at the same time to understand it and know how much I can demand of it in any situation.

The exercises I learned with Paula accompany me until this day, and during periods when I fail to do them and do not observe the basic body-maintenance rules of proper contractions, proper sitting, etc. — old and new pains appear at once.

That is why I see Sphincter Gymnastics as a way of life and a means of living at peace with our bodies.

Rona — General Improvement

I came to Paula for treatment at the age of 40. My reason was that from a very early age, even before I bore children, I had a protruding abdomen. After some time of treatment, I began to feel changes starting in my body with regard to things I had never related to until then.

1. I had suffered from short-windedness since I was very young. This went away during the treatment.

2. From an early age I had a 'crooked' back, and at an early age took part in orthopedic gymnastics at school, which didn't help. After a time of treatment with Paula I got a 'straight' back.

3. I was used to having to go to the bathroom at least once or twice at night. This, too, went away.

4. My abdomen pulled in, my buttocks got slimmer, my thighs got slimmer, and so did the upper part of my body.

5. As to my face — creases I had alongside my nose have smoothed out, and the cheek muscles have lifted.

6. I hadn't felt my big toes for a long time. When I touched them they had no sensation. One day I suddenly realized that the feeling had come back in my big toes — just like the rest of the toes.

7. A lump on the back of my neck disappeared.

8. My right arm used to 'fall asleep' — this, too, stopped happening.

Erela — General Improvement

I started treatment in October 1976.

Reasons for treatment:

I came for treatment because of a general feeling of laxity (poor posture) and a desire to study voice development.

Improvement in health and functioning:

1. Before treatment I suffered from very severe menstrual pains. The pains disappeared entirely after the first month of treatment.

2. I lost a great deal of blood in my periods. The amount of blood decreased as treatment progressed.

3. The duration of my periods, which was five to six days before the treatment, decreased and is now three to four days.

4. Before treatment I had suffered pains from a slipped disc: deformative changes in two vertebrae of the neck was causing acute pain in my left leg (so much so that I was dragging my leg), and the entire left side of my body used to 'seize up'. Now there is hardly any pain, and there is also considerable improvement in all the functioning of the left side.

5. I suffered from difficulty in containing myself and from frequent urination both day and night (up to five times a night!). The difficulty has disappeared, and I don't get up at night at all now.

6. Before the treatment started I had disturbances in far vision and was even tested to fit eyeglasses. My eyesight has totally improved.

7. My posture has improved, so that my chest cage has expanded and clothes from previous years are now too tight around the shoulders and chest.

8. There is great improvement in my voice production.

9. I now look fresher and prettier than before the treatment, and my general mood has changed for the better (feeling stronger and more optimistic).

Naama — General Improvement

The changes that occurred in me during treatment with Paula Garbourg were in very diverse areas.

In the wake of improved posture, changes took place throughout my body. The parts of my body and face became more correctly proportioned. My lips, for instance, became prettier, the angle of my nose changed, making it look shorter, my hair became thicker and its growth accelerated.

My menstrual pains went away, and the periods shortened from eight to five days.

My mobility has improved in terms of suppleness and fitness, I run faster, and dance better, too — also because of a considerable improvement in my sense of rhythm. This is one of the beautiful sensations I have enjoyed thanks to the treatment; a feeling of inner rhythm and inner wholeness throughout my body. The feeling of alienation between body and mind, or of an 'I' imprisoned in a body, has vanished. Everything has turned into a single whole.

Yael (Professional Singer) — General Improvement

I have been doing Sphincter Gymnastics exercises for some two and a half years. Many changes have occurred in me during this time. It is very hard for someone who has not experienced it to believe how many important things can happen through doing such simple exercises.

I can say wholeheartedly that these 'gymnastics' have changed my life in all senses.

I shall try to describe some of them:

I was a very introverted and inhibited person, and I have become more extroverted, spontaneous, and open to people.

I was very passive and a day dreamer, and today I am alert, energetic and vital, practical and productive. My independence has increased. My emotional stability has increased. My ability to concentrate has gone up amazingly, as well as my capacity for thought and study.

My belief in myself has increased, and my sense of responsibility has developed. My sleep has become much more serene.

Many physical changes have occurred, such as:

I was knock-kneed, and my legs have straightened.

My abdominal and back muscles have become stronger.

My senses have sharpened.

The muscle cramps I suffered from have stopped.

I have become much slimmer, though I eat more.

My arms, which were thin and weak, have gotten stronger.

My breathing has changed completely and become deeper.

My digestion is regular.

The menstrual pains I suffered from have stopped altogether.

As a singer, I must mention that here, too, many things have changed: my voice has become deep, fluent and round, and its volume has increased. The difficulties I suffered from, such as reaching very high or low notes — have disappeared.

My stage fright has vanished, too.

My capacity for self-expression is much greater, and musical and emotional expression is easier for me.

My singing itself is much more flowing and voice production is effortless.

I am much freer on the stage.

These are only part of the changes.

I'll conclude with my great thanks to Paula Garbourg, who developed this method. For me, this has been one of the most important things that has happened to me in my life — if not the most important.

Letter from a Patient Who Became an Instructor of the Paula Garbourg Method

I should like to give my opinion on a number of important points:

A. Paula Garbourg's method is not miraculous. If you don't work, there won't be results. As your perseverance grows, inner treasures you didn't know existed will turn up. If you are lax — warning signals will flash. Problems will threaten to re-attach themselves to you.

B. Paula Garbourg's method does not depend on the instructor's personality. That is, while the method would of course not exist were it not for its inventor (or more correctly, its first discoverer), the charismatic qualities of the instructor have only a limited effect on the success of the treatment. Certain patients are decidedly reserved in their personal relations with those teaching the method, but nevertheless utilize it to the full. Furthermore, the treatment leads directly up to total disengagement from the instructor, without any deliberate effort being made to that end. This independence was one of the points that impressed me most. Continents away and with no correspondence related to the treatment, I kept progressing on my own throughout the years that elapsed since then. It is superfluous to add that this method has none of the hallmarks of suggestion. Of all the movement methods I have known, and I have known quite a few, this is the 'driest'.

C. The method does not change the person. It only peels away what is superfluous, and corrects the equilibrium in the totality of phenomena of which he is composed.

D. The parallel between the mental and the physical results is truly incredible — like a mathematical parallel.

E. And this is the most important point. In my opinion, the method is 'right'. That is, every part of it proves, practically and automatically, the validity of all the rest of its parts. Of all the things I have tried and experienced — there has never been any contradiction between one detail and another in the totality of the exercises. It may even be said that if there existed a student or patient who had achieved an ideal state, any one of the entire range of exercises he might perform would produce as its final stage a result identical to that of any other exercise.

130

PART III
EXERCISES

Preface

The Sphincter Gymnastics method does not insist on a specific way to perform the exercises and does not demand a predetermined goal that must be achieved through them. It isn't the number of exercises that matters, but the benefit the body derives from each one. Each person executes the exercises in the specific manner suitable to him/her, according to his/her physical capabilities and as he/she wishes.

Nobody knows just what is going on in someone else's body, how an illness was produced, or why this or that muscle has contracted or slackened. Only the body knows, and only it can restore itself to proper condition. For every single case, various exercises are given, the task of which is to spur the body back to harmony and competence. Sometimes it happens surprisingly fast, but it can also take a long time.

Just as one must train to achieve in sports, so, too, must one train to make the body sound again. *The body must be re-educated* to normal performance: walking, sitting, lying, standing, eating and drinking must be re-learned in order to return to natural harmony.

Just as physical defects do not appear from one day to the next, so too, good physical condition does not return overnight, but rather gradually. It takes time and patience to succeed.

In cases of infirm health, the exercises should be done only with a doctor's approval and under supervision.

The following descriptions of the exercises are based on an optimum course for each one. Specific to each individual, the exercises appear entirely different at the initial learning stages to many of the persons being treated. In the later stages of performance, the exercises match the descriptions presented in this section.

Sphincter Gymnastics

Sphincter Gymnastics is performed on a special bed: a 6 cm thick foam-rubber mattress, on a wooden board about 3 cm thick. In the absence of that kind of bed in the house, spreading a mattress or blanket on the floor will do.

A large proportion of the exercises can be performed almost anywhere and in any situation: sitting, standing or walking, in the course of work, travel or recreation. In this way, Sphincter Gymnastics becomes a part of one's ordinary life.

The Effect of the Lower Sphincters on the System

In my 50 years of working with the sphincters, certain interactions among them became clear to me. I would initially like to consider some effects of the two lower sphincters on the entire system. It will be remembered that for brevity's sake we are calling the sphincter of the urinary duct the front sphincter, and that of the anus the rear sphincter.

— The effect of the rear sphincter is to enable the spine to bend backward.
— The effect of the front sphincter is to enable the spine to turn forward.
— The combined effect of both sphincters is to enable the spine to straighten.
— Both lower sphincters activate the feet in walking, dancing, running and jumping.
— In sitting down, the front sphincter is activated.
— In standing up, the rear sphincter is activated.
— The front sphincter assists in sitting up from a reclining position and vice versa.

— The effect of the rear sphincter is to make it possible to bend to the right and to the left.
— The effect of the front sphincter is to make it possible to turn to the right and to the left.
— Front-sphincter action makes the toes and feet move towards the leg (Dorsal Flexion).
— Rear-sphincter action makes the toes and feet move into line with the leg (Plantar Flexion).
— The effect of the lower sphincters is to turn the head from side to side.
— The effect of the front sphincter is to spread the fingers and raise the hands.
— The effect of the rear sphincter is to clench the fists and bend the elbows.
— The effect of the lower sphincters is to open and close the eyelids.
— The effect of the front sphincter is to turn the eyes to the right and to the left.
— The effect of the lower sphincters is to open and close the nostrils.
— The rear sphincter makes it possible to move the scalp at the crown of the head, while the front sphincter makes it possible to move the scalp above the forehead.
— The effect of the lower sphincters is to open and close the mouth and contract and relax the lips.
— The lower sphincters govern voice production.

The reciprocal effect among the lower sphincters and the other parts of the body, though it always exists, is somewhat disturbed when the sphincters aren't working properly. This reciprocal effect can therefore only be sensed distinctly by someone whose sphincter action is good or has been made so by the Sphincter Gymnastics method.

While the selection of exercises described below is not exhaustive, it provides an idea of just what the technique of Sphincter Gymnastics is.

Three Basic Exercises for the Lower Sphincters

— Contracting and relaxing in regular rhythm.
— Double contractions, the second stronger than the first.
— Contractions in rapid sequence, without any relaxing.
These exercises may be done with either of the lower sphincters (front or rear) or with both at the same time.
The exercises may be done in each of the following positions:
Lying on the back with knees drawn up to the chest.
Lying on the back with the knees bent and feet planted parallel on the bed.
Lying on the back with legs straight.
It is also possible to do the exercises lying on the stomach in various positions. This, however, requires trained assistance.
The arms usually rest alongside the body.

Basic Front-Sphincter Exercises

A. Lying on Back, Knees Drawn up to Chest
1. *Contracting and relaxing in regular rhythm:* In this position, when the front sphincter is contracted the small of the back pushes down on the mattress and the pelvis lifts and pulls slightly towards the chest. When the sphincter relaxes, the pelvis drops lightly back to the starting point. The result is a sort of pelvic swing, powered by the front sphincter's contracting and relaxing.

2. *Double contractions, the second stronger than the first:*
The contractions make the small of the back push down on the
mattress more and more. In the very slight interval between the
two contractions, a slight relaxation occurs naturally even if an
attempt is made to maintain the contraction. At the time of this
minimal relaxation the pelvis moves, but only slightly, towards
the starting point.

3. *Contractions in rapid sequence, without any relaxing:*
This exercise makes the pelvis lift more and more towards the
chest. Young people trained in the Sphincter Gymnastics
technique will feel, as the pelvis lifts, the legs straightening and
being pulled towards the head until the feet actually touch the
mattress above the head — the entire movement being powered
by the increasingly strong contractions of the front sphincter.

B. Lying on Back with Feet Planted Parallel

1. *Contracting and relaxing in regular rhythm:* When the
front sphincter is contracted in this position, with the feet planted

parallel, the small of the back pushes down on the mattress, the pelvis lifts and is drawn to the chest, the raised knees move towards each other, and the heels move away from each other. When the sphincter is relaxed and the pelvis goes back to its starting position, the knees move away from each other and fall a little to the sides, the big toes move a little away from each other and the heels move together to the same extent. In this position, the pelvic swing is smaller than when lying on the back with the knees drawn up to the chest.

2. *Double contractions, the second stronger than the first:* With each contraction the small of the back pushes down on the mattress more and more. The lordosis at the small of the back flattens, knees and big toes move towards each other, heels move apart and the pelvis lifts slightly.

3. *Contractions in rapid sequence, without any relaxing:* The pelvis lifts slowly until there is a straight line slanting down from knees to shoulders. The entire movement is powered by the contraction of the front sphincter.

C. Lying on Back with Legs Straight

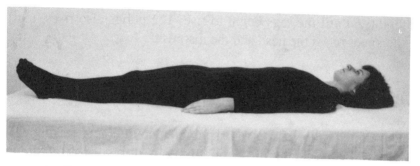

1. *Contracting and relaxing in regular rhythm:* The legs rotate inwards and are stretched, the big toes move together and the feet bend up towards the shin (Dorsal Flexion).

2. *Double contractions, the second stronger than the first:* The legs rotate inwards, the knees flatten more and more, the feet bend towards the shin (Dorsal Flexion), the spine straightens, and the lordosis becomes very flat.

Feet bent up towards shin in Dorsal Flexion.

3. Contractions in rapid sequence, without any relaxation:
The legs rotate inwards. With each contraction the knees bend slightly, until the legs begin to rise. The pelvis also rises, until the knees reach the head and the mattress.

Basic Rear-Sphincter (Anus) Exercises

A.
The contraction of the rear sphincter counteracts raising the knees. There is therefore no point in doing rear-sphincter exercises in the first position of lying on the back with knees drawn up to chest. We shall, then, go on to the basic rear-sphincter exercises in the second position.

B. Lying on Back with Feet Planted Parallel

The toes and feet straighten in line with the legs (Plantar Flexion).

1. *Contracting and relaxing in regular rhythm:* Upon contracting, the small of the back pushes down, the knees part and the heels move towards each other. Upon relaxing, the pelvis drops back and knees and heels return to the starting position. Owing to these movements that originate in the rear sphincter, the swing motion is generated here, as well.

2. *Double contractions, the second stronger than the first:* With each contraction the small of the back is pushed down more strongly. The pelvis does not lift. The knees part more and more, and the heels move towards each other. When maximum spreading of the knees is reached with the exercise, the reverse exercise, i.e, double contractions of the front sphincter with a slight interval between the double contractions (see exercise B(2) on p. 138), should be done until the knees are pressed together. Repeat this sequence several times.

3. *Contractions in rapid sequence without any relaxation:* The pelvis lifts little by little until a straight line is produced, slanting down from knees to shoulders. The knees part and the heels come closer together.

C. *Lying on Back with Legs Straight*
1. *Contracting and relaxing in regular rhythm:* The legs rotate outward. The toes and feet straighten in line with the legs (Plantar Flexion).

2. *Double contractions, the second stronger than the first:* The legs rotate outward. The toes and feet straighten very strongly in line with the legs (Plantar Flexion). The spine straightens more and more

3. *Contractions in rapid sequence without any relaxation:* The legs rotate outward. The pelvis lifts, the legs and thighs stretch. The toes and feet stretch out in line with the legs (Plantar

Flexion). When this exercise is at its peak, the whole body arches from shoulders to feet.

Basic Exercises for Both Lower (Front and Rear) Sphincters Performed Simultaneously

A.

The reclining position with knees drawn up to the chest is not relevant for these exercises either. We shall therefore proceed to the exercises in the second position.

B. Lying on Back with Feet Planted Parallel

1. *Contracting and relaxing in regular rhythm:* The entire spine is flush against the mattress. The big toes, heels and knees are together. There is no pelvic swing.

2. *Double contractions, the second stronger than the first:* The spine straightens, the lordosis becomes flatter, the big toes, heels and knees are together.

3. *Contractions in rapid sequence without any relaxation:* The legs are together, toes and feet stretched in line with the legs (Plantar Flexion). The spine is utterly straight, the lordosis flat.

Note About Lower Sphincter Exercises

It is always a good idea to begin and end an exercise session with the front sphincter.

The rear sphincter, which consists of two ring muscles — an interior and an exterior one — is usually stronger than the front sphincter and needs to be exercised about half as much. Activating both the back muscles and the abdominal muscles

142

pulls the shoulders forcibly back through the trapezius muscle, and increases the lordosis at the small of the back, creating a hollow. This is not a normal or comfortable posture, and cannot be tolerated for long.

When the rear sphincter is dominant, aggressiveness appears. The heels are drawn together, body weight rests on the front of the foot, and the facial expression becomes belligerent. This stance, sometimes caused by high-heeled shoes, produces a sway back and tips the edge of the upper pelvis forward. Driving a car, with the legs always spread, also makes the rear sphincter work more and tends to produce a sway back.

It may well be that overactivity of the rear sphincter is also a cause of the lumbago that is so prevalent; as well as of discus hernia which, among other things, causes a loss of sensation around the genitals with a resulting lack of bladder control and disturbances in sexual intercourse. Exercise No. 2 for combatting asymmetry (see p. 147), may be helpful in such cases. 'The Hands on Eyes' exercise on p. 164 also helps in certain instances.

When doing front sphincter exercises, lying on the back with the knees pulled up to the abdomen makes it easier to keep the rear sphincter from working at the same time, as often happens at first. (Of course all the sphincters do work simultaneously, but it should be possible to activate them separately.) When lying on the back with the feet planted parallel, pressing the big toes and the knees together achieves the same purpose and makes it easier to sense the front sphincter. (For the effect of the heels and big toes, see p. 137).

The front sphincter can also be exercised with relative ease sitting down. With the big toes and the knees pressed together it is easy to feel the front sphincter, and it may be exercised without

143

difficulty in very slight contracting and relaxing movements. This makes the body straighten up into an erect sitting posture.

Exercising and strengthening the front sphincter also affects the rear sphincter. We know from experience that a prolapse of the rectum should not be treated by exercising the rear sphincter itself. It is necessary, as explained on p. 148, to begin with eyelid exercises. In this way improvement may be achieved indirectly, as is so often the case in Sphincter Gymnastics.

Everyday Acts Applied as Sphincter Gymnastics Exercises

Standing and Sitting

There are everyday acts that provide excellent sphincter exercise when they are performed correctly. Performing these everyday acts correctly is a way of exercising that does not take time.

To stand straight, the heels, big toes, calves, knees and thighs should be drawn together. This contracts the lower sphincters and allows them to influence posture.

Bowlegged people can't bring their knees together. In that event the knees should be bent slightly forward until they can touch. This straightens the body. Bowleggedness can be reduced by sphincter exercises. Bowlegged people usually have widely separated shoulder blades. In mild cases, pulling the shoulder blades together pulls the knees together as well. In severe cases (many of them athletes), the mouth and other sphincters should be exercised.

It is also possible to straighten up in a seated position. The

chair should be without springs, and all four legs of equal height.
Attention should be paid that there is a right angle:
between the pelvis and the thighs
between the thighs and the calves
between the calves and the feet.
In correct sitting, the heels and big toes should be together, as well as the calves, knees and thighs.

Sitting down and Standing up

Sitting down and getting up are the lower sphincters' jobs. In sitting down, the front sphincter operates, that is, it contracts and relaxes. To sit down correctly, the legs should be about parallel, the feet turned slightly in, and the knees bent. The body slowly drops straight into the chair without the buttocks lifting or protruding and without increased curvature at the small of the back.

To stand up correctly, the feet should be turned slightly outwards with the heels together, making it easier to contract the rear sphincter. This makes it possible to stand up almost without bending forward, leaning hands on thighs, pushing oneself out of the chair, or thrusting the buttocks up and out.

Lying down Correctly

Health permitting, the best way to lie down is without a pillow under the head.

Anyone used to lying on one side should do so on his or her dominant side. If one is accustomed to working, writing, engaging in sports, etc. with only one hand — in the course of time the body will lean towards the same side. When lying down, the leg on that side should be as straight as possible, without force, and in contrast the other leg should be bent as much as possible. Balance of the pelvis is achieved by this position.

Lying down correctly as described above not only serves to restore balance, it also makes it easier to fall asleep. The equilibrium achieved reduces tensions in the pelvis and elsewhere in the body.

Exercises for Asymmetry

Exercise A

As already mentioned, most people suffer from asymmetry in their bodies as a result of the dominant use of one hand. The active hand usually stays half closed, as does the eye on that side. The dominant side of the body is, in fact, more contracted than the other.

To remedy this, we must do the opposite of our everyday habits.

A right-handed person should spread the four fingers of the right hand as much as he/she can. The thumb will do what it needs without assistance. A left-handed person should do the same thing with the fingers of his/her left hand. This position should be held for some time. It is liable to hurt, but that is a sign that the exercise is, in fact, needed. After a relatively short time it is possible to feel the body straightening out. This straightening initiates from the lower sphincters. The abdomen lifts. People whose right hand is dominant will feel the lower jaw move towards the right, the more contracted right eye opens wider, and the right eyebrow — which is often lower than the left — returns to its proper level.

People who suffer from shoulder and arm pains can often obtain swift relief by doing this exercise with the dominant hand. The effect radiates all over that half of the body, from head to toe. That side of the body straightens first, and the other after it. Sometimes the process takes longer.

Exercise B

This exercise has an especially powerful effect on the equilibrium, and can sometimes help with severe backaches:

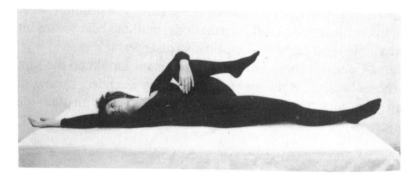

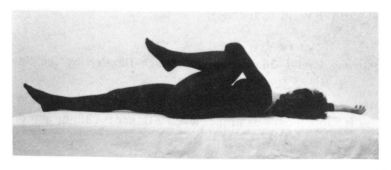

The patient lies on his/her back on the exercise bed described earlier. If the right side is dominant, the left leg is bent, pulled to the chest, and clasped to the abdomen by the left elbow. The right leg remains straight and stretched out as much as possible. The right arm is raised above the head until the back of the right hand rests on the mattress. In this position, the head is turned right and upwards until the palm of the right hand can be seen.

In this position the body is considerably stretched. Unpracticed people will certainly experience pain. In many cases, the patient may soon feel the body heating up at the site of the pain. A feeling of whirlpool-like flow is generated at that spot. The painful area heats up more, reddens.

Sometimes the heat will roam from one place to another until it finally reaches the source of the pain. The position should be maintained, with brief interruptions, until the heat passes and then — in most cases — the pain also disappears.

A person whose left hand is dominant should do the same exercise with the right leg bent, the left leg extended, raising the left arm, and turning the face to the left, i.e., with the sides reversed.

Eye and Eyelid Exercises

A. Strong Eyelid Contraction as though Dazzled by the Sun

Strong contraction of the eyelids is a reflexive reaction to pain.

It happens, for example, when a finger is caught in a door.

The eyelids can actually be felt to contract very strongly, as does the body, because now all the sphincter muscles are working simultaneously.

In contrast with sudden pain — any sudden shock makes the mouth gape and the eyes open wide. In that case, the eyelids should be contracted as strongly as possible. This makes the sphincter muscles contract and go back to normal functioning, causing the paralysis of faculties brought on by the shock to recede.

Contracting the eyelids helps relieve sudden pain, as that caused by a fall or blow. It does not help with pain arising from illness. In cases of sudden pain, eyelid exercises are a good point of departure for mobilizing the entire system, and causing the pain to pass.

This exercise has additional aspects. It sometimes helps make a rigid spine move and recover its flexibility. One lies on the back, knees drawn up to chest, hands laced, clasping the knees. The eyelids are then contracted strongly, as though against very dazzling sunlight. When the eyelids relax after a while, they are again contracted for as long as possible. During all this time the eyes are not opened even when the eyelids relax from the contraction. This operation is repeated several times. It is a great effort, but leaves behind a pleasant feeling of release.

Contracting the eyelids correctly does not make the eyes hurt. If there is, nevertheless, pain, the exercise should be stopped immediately, and the eyes covered with the palms. Only after the pain has passed is it permissible to resume the exercise. *This exercise should not be done without medical approval.*

After the exercise has been repeated several times, the eyes are covered by the hands and the body is now allowed to move as it likes. After some time, it is possible to start again. The number of repeats depends on individual condition, as the exercise involves great exertion. If one has ever had the feeling that the body is a single, whole entity — this exercise will provide confirmation.

The exercise can be done in various positions. The choice of position may be different in each case and may in each case yield different results. A practiced person who does this exercise lying on his/her back might, for instance, feel the trunk of the body tending to lift up of its own volition. The very same exercise, however, may sometimes make the legs fold up towards the abdomen. This exercise, like all the other exercises, acts in accord with the body's needs and assumes different forms each time.

It must be stressed that this exercise should be performed only by young, healthy people. Medical approval and supervision of specially trained instructors is required for elderly people to do this exercise.

B. Contracting and Relaxing the Eyelids

A very good point of departure for normalizing the body. Unlike Exercise A, the motion this time is delicate and continuous, like the eyelid movement that occurs in sleep. This exercise has a most soothing effect. If performed at bedtime, it makes it easier to fall asleep; but if done for any length of time as part of a workout, it arouses the whole system into action.

People suffering from bladder incontinence, asthma, insomnia, sinusitis, prolapse, hypermotority in children, backaches and other complaints, have reported that this exercise sometimes led to getting rid of the complaint, and in other cases, considerably relieved their suffering.

150

C. Vigorous Closing and Opening of the Eyes

This movement, which seems so natural and matter of course, is surprisingly difficult for many people. This difficulty can be removed by exercise, though doing so entails great exertion. It is not recommended for the aged. The exercise affects the spine and the cervical and lumbar lordoses, and consequently the body's overall equilibrium. People who suffer from constipation have reported that this exercise benefitted their digestive system, and that complete or partial normalization of their bowel movements resulted.

D. "Eyes Falling into Head"

One should close one's eyes lightly and imagine them falling freely, easily into the head — as though through empty space — and coming back, freely and easily through that empty space, to where they belong (a sort of yo-yo motion may be imagined). This exercise should be done as freely and easily as possible, and in a slow rhythm. It is preferable to do it lying down, even on a lawn. The classic movement of opening and closing, contracting and relaxing, is produced. This exercise is very relaxing, and incidentally stimulates one sphincter after the other, stretches the body and makes it erect.

E. Eyelids Gently Pressing Eyes

The eyelids gently press the eyes into the head. The pressure of the eyelids on the eyes is like the gentle pressure of a flattened palm against a wall — the way a mother rests her hand on her child's forehead.

This very gentle pressure of the eyelids (it is not a contraction) makes the lordosis very flat. The working of the urinary tract's sphincter intensifies. The fingers and toes spread. The feet are pushed towards the shin (Dorsal Flexion). The fingers are pushed backwards towards the arm.

This is not a relaxation exercise. On the contrary. Since the lordosis becomes unusually flat, the effect is very strong. It pulls the whole body erect.

This exercise also requires medical approval and trained supervision.

F. Looking from Ear to Ear

The two index fingers are placed lightly and without pressure on the tragus of the ears, and an attempt is made to 'look', without straining, from ear to ear (from tragus to tragus). Of course one can not see one's own ears, but the movement should imply an attempt to do so.

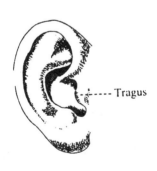

Tragus

In the event of discomfort, or mild pain in the eyes, the exercise should be interrupted. To relieve the discomfort, the hands are placed on the eyes and a brief rest ensues. When the discomfort passes, the exercise is resumed, first looking from left to right and then from right to left. If possible, the head remains immobile and does not follow the movement of the eyes. The fingers on the ears serve only to provide direction. After a time, when one is sure of the direction, they may be removed from the ears.

The exercise is done first with the eyes open, and later with closed eyes.

The exercise has a highly relaxing effect, sometimes even inducing sleep. People suffering from polyps and injured vocal cords have reported that this exercise affected their condition beneficially.

Mouth Exercises

A. Upper Lip to Nose

In this exercise the upper lip is pushed towards the nose. Both the lower lip and the chin should be employed to accomplish this. The chin is the prop that pushes the lower lip up. The lower lip in turn pushes the upper lip, which curls widely upwards towards the nose. This should be done without making the lower jaw jut forward in the process.

The 'Upper Lip to Nose' exercise makes the respiratory and abdominal muscles work, and with them the long muscles of the back, the rear and front sphincters, and ultimately the entire body.

During the exercise the upper lip should be spread widely as it curls broadly upwards. This is a relaxing position.

If the upper lip is contracted when it folds upward, the effect is the opposite. We become nervous and even aggressive, since contracting the upper lip causes the lower lip, as well as the rear sphincter, to contract. In contrast, an upper lip that is spread widely when it folds upward has a relaxing effect, because it activates the front sphincter.

This exercise has various effects.

Sphincter Gymnastics experience has shown that a person suffering from acute asthma is incapable of performing the 'Upper Lip to Nose' exercise. Asthmatics often have increased lordoses of the neck and small of the back. So when an asthmatic gets to the stage where he can push his upper lip to his nose, it is a sign that he's on the road to recovery.

When the upper lip is pushed towards the nose, the nose opens. The exercise is effective against coughing; the neck and throat are relaxed, the coughing decreases, the breathing becomes deeper, and powers of concentration improve.

The 'Upper Lip to Nose' exercise has a direct effect on the shoulder zone. The shoulders are pulled back, the rib cage lifts, the windpipe is relaxed and breathing becomes easier. The effect also reaches the back muscles, which begin to work more vigorously, thereby providing the link between the back and the pelvis.

When the chin pushes the lower lip against the upper, and the upper is pushed by the lower towards the nose, the lordosis of the neck decreases. This in turn affects the lordosis at the small of the back through the back muscles. The pelvis straightens and its contents slowly return to their normal position, no longer pressing forward and pulling down. People who suffer from various kinds of prolapses therefore report great improvement in their condition and sometimes total disappearance of the anomalous defect. The exercise is relaxing, and reduces pulling at the small of the back and pressure on the legs.

Pains in the lower back are sometimes an indication that the contents of the pelvis are tipped forward; very painful pressure is being exerted on the spine near the small of the back. Practicing the 'Upper Lip to Nose' exercise reduces the pressure on the spine, as well as that on the legs. The legs return to a normal position of their own accord. The walk changes and becomes lighter. The weight of body no longer bears down on the legs, since the upper part of the pelvis is not tipped forward any more.

With the pelvis again in a normal position, the lordosis at the small of the back decreases, the bladder functions more vigorously, and urinating becomes easier.

This exercise also has a beneficial effect on the digestion. The same is true for various types of headaches, where the effect can even be very speedy.

Floor washing is strenuous, exhausting, irritating work for many women. There is an answer for that. If a toothpick is held between the upper lip and the nose, the job can be done without effort or irritation. It turns out that washing floors doesn't have to be all that hard. The toothpick must be held between the upper lip and the nose uninterruptedly, so that the exercise is being performed all the time the work is in progress. Otherwise the muscles of the upper lip will slacken again, the exercise will not have been performed correctly, and it will fail to have any beneficial effect.

In reading, writing, studying, or any other occupation that demands concentrating, even doing a crossword puzzle, this exercise is likely to enhance powers of concentration. It also has a beneficial effect on the strength and agility of the fingers in activities, such as playing the piano.

In lifting a heavy object, or in pushing something heavy, the mouth is instinctively brought into the 'Upper Lip to Nose' position. Here too, holding a toothpick will make the job easier.

And finally, it is hard to be angry or excited while performing the 'Upper Lip to Nose' exercise. We become relaxed, and react calmly.

B. "Oo-ee'

This is a clearcut opening and closing exercise. To perform it, the sounds 'oo—ee, oo—ee, oo—ee' are enunciated alternately. The 'oo' (as in 'mood') is produced with a strong contraction of the lips — to the utmost limit. The 'ee' (as in 'fleet') is produced by expanding the mouth, also to the utmost. The exercise is performed by shifting the mouth from extreme contraction to extreme expansion. This has a strong normalizing effect on all the sphincters. The back and abdominal muscles work alternatively.

Obviously, action and effect of the exercise differ for different people. With one person it elicits soft, gentle movements, in another — strong movements. And in a third it produces movements that are almost a dance. Sometimes there is a feeling of cramps being released inside the body, or of the body stretching or contracting greatly, etc. The possibilities are infinite. Each body responds according to its own needs.

Almost all the participants perform this exercise with great gusto. The exercise should not be kept up until fatigue sets in, but only as long as it is pleasant.

The 'Oo-ee' exercise releases many tensions, thereby affecting stability and balance.

The exercise is begun lying down. Later it may be performed standing up. When standing, the body works even more vigorously. The exercise can also be performed sitting down.

Due to the many types of results produced, this exercise can only be explained in a general way. Sometimes its effect is just the opposite of what is expected. The body arrives at the correct result in its own way.

C. Contracting and Relaxing the Lips

The lips are contracted slightly towards the center of the mouth — and then relaxed. It is a small movement made without force or effort. Though the movement is almost imperceptible, the effect is very strong. There is a similarity between this exercise and that in which the eyelids are contracted and relaxed.

This is one of the easier and more pleasant exercises; pleasant because of the rather rapid responses. Reaction is almost always felt in some part of the body. This exercise acts beneficially on all the sphincters of the face, on the lower sphincters, the feet, the hands, and the whole body.

Though it is a relatively easy exercise, it can be quite exerting and should not be overdone.

D. Prolonged 'Sh'

It is a simple and very effective exercise to produce a long drawn out shushing sound: 'sh-sh-sh-sh-sh-sh-sh-sh'.

How is a child soothed? The mother says 'sh-sh-sh' until the child calms down. The mother relaxes at the same time, for the shushing sound soothes both her and the child.

The exercise should be performed effortlessly. It is soothing and makes extended breathing possible. 'Sh-sh' may be hummed very quietly when alone, while working, taking a walk, etc. It is almost inaudible and highly effective. It is relaxing while driving a car, and makes for clear thinking.

Sometimes the exercise affects the eyes greatly. The eyelids contract, making the front sphincter contract, as well. This is one of the reasons for its beneficial effect.

The link between the eyes and the front sphincter (both of which are affected by this exercise) is suggested by the fact that people suffering from lack of control in urinating or from other ailments associated with the sphincter of the urinary duct often suffer from eye disorders, as well. Even people with healthy eyes complain of veiled vision. Once they can again control urination, i.e. the front sphincter is working normally, faulty sight arising from this often clears up.

The 'Sh' exercise has a beneficial effect on the lordoses. When the lordosis of the neck becomes normal, it stops exerting pressure on the neck vertebrae. This, too, is good for the eyes. The eyelids can again open and close, contract and relax correctly.

In doing the 'Sh' exercise, care should be taken that the upper lip does not contract, but broadens as it curls upward. A contracted upper lip elicits a reverse response, exciting rather than calming.

While doing the 'Sh' exercise, one must not think about breathing. An eagerness to breathe 'correctly' makes for unnatural breathing. Breathing — the basis of all life — is a spontaneous, involuntary, unlearned action, requiring no deliberate control or direction if the respiratory muscles are in good working order. Correct breathing therefore depends primarily on the strength and integration of the entire sphincter muscle system, and the 'Sh' exercise helps it work.

Emitting a long drawn-out 'Sh' sound causes the front sphincter to contract. This contraction goes through the entire body from the front sphincter up. The muscles can be felt contracting, starting in the pelvis and going progressively higher (it works differently for each person). The abdominal muscles are in particular affected by this contracting action. The chest and shoulders, back, legs, arms and head all join in. Ultimately, all the sphincter muscles are at work, straightening the entire body. The sequence differs in almost every case, depending on the level of contraction or slackness of the muscles. State of health, age and other individual factors also play a role. Sometimes only a short period of performing this exercise is enough to make one feel relief and even real improvement.

People suffering from various kinds of prolapse, varicose veins, or hemorrhoids, have reported that the 'Prolonged Sh' helped them a great deal, sometimes even within quite a short time.

Here is another effect:

To open a cramped hand or fingers, to straighten or lift an affected arm or leg, it is sometimes enough to sound a long and easy 'Sh' — and the cramped muscles loosen up.

Neither this nor the following exercise should be done by people suffering from asthma.

Combined Exercise: Prolonged 'Sh' and Front Sphincter

In many cases it is impossible to begin exercising with direct action of the front sphincter, because the person exercising doesn't control or even feel the front sphincter. After the eyelid exercise or the 'Prolonged Sh' however, the front sphincter begins functioning.

For young people it is best to lie on the back with the legs raised up to the abdomen. (Elderly people should do the exercise lying on the back with feet planted parallel.) The hands are placed on the knees, if possible, and the shushing sound is begun — with small, regular pauses. If the muscles are not too slack, it is immediately possible to feel very slight contractions and relaxations of the front sphincter in rhythm with the 'sh'.

Together with the 'sh' we begin to deliberately and very slightly contract and relax the front sphincter as though controlling an urge to urinate. Simultaneity is produced between the mouth contractions and relaxations and those of the front sphincter. In the process, the abdomen contracts in an upward direction, and then relaxes. The legs move towards the abdomen and away from it in the same rhythm.

After a while, when the front sphincter is distinctly felt, it becomes apparent that the eyes as well as the legs, arms and hands, the mouth, the nose and the abdomen are also contracting and relaxing. This feeling proceeds upward to the chest and the head, to the back and to the shoulder zone. The upper and lower back lordoses become flatter — that is, the entire body works and becomes erect.

It is worthwhile to begin exercising the front sphincter only when the urinary ducts muscles are again felt.

People with asthma should not try to do the 'sh' exercise.

Hand Exercises

A. All Fingers to Thumb

The four fingertips are brought lightly to the tip of the thumb and held in that position. This is not easy for everyone to do. Sometimes it succeeds only after a long time and diligent exercising.

The effects of this exercise are diverse:
1. Pressing of arms against body, and legs against one another.
2. Mobilization of all sphincter muscles into action.
3. Straightening of the body.

People who have performed this exercise have reported improved concentration and corrected body equilibrium.

A person holding this position long enough may feel the fingertips moving against the thumb in rhythm with breathing, in light contracting and relaxing movements.

In Oriental countries, this way of holding the fingers may often be seen during an argument, as a characteristic gesture meaning 'Wait!' or 'Just a minute!' in a slowing, calming sense.

The 'All Fingers to Thumb' movement contracts the palm of the hand; followed by contraction of the mouth, the eyes and the lower sphincters. The sole of the foot also contracts in parallel with the palm of the hand, and the toes move towards each other.

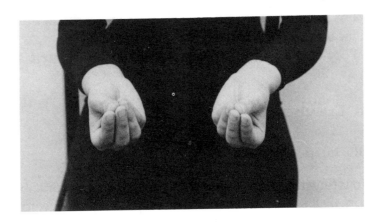

B. Each Finger Separately to Thumb

Each separate finger, starting from the little finger, is pressed lightly against the thumb — and released. This also has a beneficial effect on concentration, thinking capacity and balance. This exercise has a great many possibilities, of which we give a few variations below.

162

Four Variations

1. Move the thumb to the ring finger with the back of the hand up. This causes the front sphincter to work, and the body to straighten and stand erect. The big toes move together lightly.

2. Move the thumb to the little finger, with palm up. This causes the rear sphincter to work. The heels of the feet move towards one another.

3. Move the thumb to the index finger with back of the hand up. This exercise moves the hands forward and lifts them up, from there down to the sides of the body, and so on.

4. Press the tips of thumb and index finger together with palm up. This exercise moves the hands to the sides and up, then down again and up, and so on.

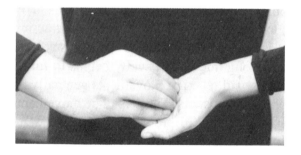

C. Fingers to Palms

The four fingertips (excluding the thumb) of each hand should simultaneously touch the middle of the palm of the opposite hand. For right-handed people, the left hand is on top and the right underneath — conversely, for left-handed people the right is

163

on top and the left underneath. The exercise causes pain or discomfort in the arms, but it soon passes. Following the exercise the body becomes erect and the feet arch. It may be performed in company, as well, since it is quite imperceptible. Children can do it in school unobserved. It will not disturb lessons, but rather enhance concentration. This exercise is good for flat feet.

D. Hands on Eyes

This is a very important exercise. The hands are placed in front of the eyes without pressure and in a manner that is comfortable. The hands also usually change position of their own volition during the exercise, finding the most individually suitable one. During this exercise, one should think of pleasant things, and not of daily problems.

Prior to this exercise a light eyelid contracting or other simple exercise can be performed. If the hands are kept in front of the eyes for long, the body usually begins to function freely with contracting and relaxing movements generally occuring in painful or problematic spots. These may be movements of limbs or organs in which painful processes began years, even many years earlier. Sometimes the body begins with almost imperceptible movements and sometimes they are very strong. They are, however, always unpremeditated. One feels cramps being released one after the other, and slack and painful muscles gradually being relaxed and growing stronger. This is the body's self-help.

The exercise is usually performed lying down. But in certain cases, particularly with old people, it may be done seated at a table. In the seated position, the torso should be at right angles to the thighs, the thighs at right angles to the legs, and the legs at right angles to the feet (see p. 144). The elbows should lean on a table high enough to make it possible to cover the eyes without bending forward, and low enough to do so without raising the shoulders. The abdomen should be as close as possible to the table.

I started using this exercise many years ago. As with the other exercises, it came of its own accord. And like all the others, it is done with contractions and relaxations. It is a movement of the sphincters. When the hands are placed in front of the eyes, the eyelids begin to contract and relax.

Tongue Exercises

A. Narrow Tongue

The tongue is connected to the sphincters of the throat and gullet (pharynx).

In the 'Narrow Tongue' exercise, the tongue is narrowed by reducing its width without curling it. The tongue stays inside the space of the mouth bordering on the teeth. It should not be between the teeth, and should not pass the lips. The lips are slightly contracted, but not pursed.

People used to walking with spraddled legs usually have wide tongues. If they exercise quite a lot on narrowing their tongues, their legs will also come more together. It is easier to perform this exercise when the legs are brought together. It is not an easy exercise, but with work and guidance it can be mastered. 'Narrow Tongue' is important for correct speech. The speech of people whose tongues are too wide is usually heavy and sometimes unclear, as well.

165

This is the first part of the exercise. After learning to narrow the tongue, it is possible to proceed to 'Short Tongue', in which the narrowed tongue is pulled back towards the root.

This exercise must be performed under supervision and with a doctor's permission. While the exercise is being performed, the shoulders are pulled sharply back, the lordoses become flatter, the body and legs straighten, the lips contract, and little by little the exercise activates the entire body — as occurs in all sphincter exercises when performed by practiced people.

B. Wandering Tongue

The tip of the tongue moves in a circle between the teeth and the lips. The tongue is pushed past the upper incisors and inserted in the meeting place of the lips and the gums. From there the tip of the tongue is led, with light pressure, along the line joining the lips and the gums — from the middle of the upper lip to the right, and full circle back to the starting point. This is then repeated in the opposite direction. That is the first part of the exercise. The same thing is done with the middle of the lower lip as the starting point, once to the right and once to the left. There are four circles in all.

This exercise requires considerable exertion. It activates the shoulders, arms, hands, spine, pelvis and legs. It is felt from head to toe.

Care should be taken that the circular movement is not fast, but rather very slow.

C. Tongue from Side to Side

There are people who, for one reason or another, can not move their lower jaws.

To mobilize the lower jaw, the tip of the tongue touches behind the extreme left tooth of the upper jaw. From there it moves in a straight line to the extreme right tooth of the upper jaw, and back and forth at a comfortable rate.

Following the movement of the tongue, the corner of the eye on the side at which the tip of the tongue is located begins to close and contract. The entire body leans from side to side.

D. Tongue Along Palate Ridge

There are several furrows and ridges at the front of the palate. If the tongue is passed lightly from one end to the other of these furrows and ridges, the whole body tends to shift in the direction of the tongue's movement. The legs in particular rock from side to side.

A mother or nursemaid can do this exercise with a small child. This refers to very small or Down's Syndrome children who are incapable of performing exercises independently. In such cases, the mother or nursemaid passes a finger from side to side across the row of ridges and furrows.

Ear Exercises

Hand to Ear — A

This is an exercise that is suitable for small children and weak people. The palms of both hands are placed over the ears, alternating between pressing the ears lightly and relaxing the pressure. This may be kept up for some time. It is very relaxing, and at the same time fully activates all the sphincters of the body.

One finger alternately presses lightly on the tragus of the ear, and relaxes the pressure. This causes the front sphincter to contract and relax. It is a good starting point for small children and weak people. The action is effective for putting the front sphincter, and other sphincters, back into proper working order.

Sphincter-Activating Massages That Have Helped Down's Syndrome Children

Very small children, especially those with Down's Syndrome, are usually unable to do exercises by themselves. In many cases they require a massage in order to activate the sphincters — initially the front sphincter, through which the rest of the muscles can be influenced. To understand the following, a certain familiarity with the elementary concepts of massage is necessary. Obviously, such massage can only be given by someone who has been trained.

On the basis of experience, the following massages are suggested:

1. The abdomen is massaged with upward strokes. The knees begin to bend, and the bent legs lift up. The children enjoy the massage, as well as the bending movements, some of which they were never able to do before.

2. The adductors (the muscles that draw the legs together) are stroked next (always in an upward direction).

3. The legs are alternately pressed together and parted again, with patting motions. Begin and finish this massage with patting the legs together.

4. The child's legs are held pressed together.

5. The child's legs are alternately raised and lowered.

6. The sole of the foot is stroked with one or two fingers, from the heel to the tips of the toes.

7. The outsides and insides of the legs are massaged with upward strokes.

8. Play 'Round Round the Garden'. with one finger stirring in the child's palm.

9. Light finger taps in the child's palm.

10. The child's thumb is brought together with the middle or ring finger.

11. All four of the child's fingers are brought together with the thumb.

12. The fingers are lifted with light pressure towards the back of the hand.

13. The lips are stroked with the thumb and forefinger, from the corners of the mouth toward the middle.

14. The same with the cheeks, using thumb and forefinger.

15. The nostrils are pressed together gently (from the tip of the nose), and relaxed and pressed again; and repeat.

16. The eyebrows are stroked lightly from the temples towards the bridge of the nose and back; and repeat.

17. The forehead is massaged lightly with downward and upward strokes.

18. The bridge of the nose is massaged with upward strokes, and then with downward strokes. The strokes are very gentle, without force, using one or two fingers — depending on the width of the bridge of the nose.

19. The palms of the hands are placed over the child's ears, pressed lightly to the head, and then released. This exercise, like all the others, is one of contraction and relaxation; that is, it stimulates sphincter movement.

20. The tragus of the child's ear is pressed lightly with one finger and then released.

21. The child's hands are placed over its eyes. This may be done for only a rather short time at first so that the child will not be frightened by the sudden darkness. In time, the child becomes willing to leave its hands in front of its eyes for longer. It is best to cover the child's hands with one's own. This may be done with the child lying in bed. It is even better to hold the child on one's lap with its hands on its own eyes — and incidentally to talk to the child. Then the child is not afraid and the exercise can proceed.

22. The 'peek-a-boo' game that is played with small children — covering and uncovering the eyes — is also based on natural sphincter movement: contracting and relaxing, closing and opening.

23. When children bang the crowns of their heads or their foreheads against a wall, it is desirable in many cases to give a vigorous massage. The child's head is held between the hands, one hand at the side of the forehead and the other at the back of the head. Quite strong up-and-down movements are then made with the hands. We have observed that children particularly like this massage.

24. The forehead is stroked quite vigorously from the temples towards the middle, then lightly back to the temples; and repeat. This exercise brings the front and rear sphincters into action, and has a relaxing and calming effect.

25. Light pats on the back between the shoulder-blades (at

the spot that many children bang against the wall) are soothing, and all children like it. (Every mother does this to soothe her child).

26. Light pats on the forehead are particularly effective with children who bang their foreheads against hard things.

While the exercises described in this book seem simple, it should be borne in mind that they are part of an independent exercise method that is not integrative with other gymnastic methods. Sphincter Gymnastics is a re-education of the body. It is possible to engage in other types of sports and gymnastics only after order has been restored in the body by Sphincter Gymnastics. In any event, this should not be done simultaneously with Sphincter Gymnastics. Any other exercise will hinder the course of the body's normalization. It is never a good idea to combine a number of gymnastic methods, and even less so with Sphincter Gymnastics. This is because *Sphincter Gymnastics is based on a single principle: that all the sphincters work together simultaneously, contracting in unison and relaxing in unison.* It is this we must concentrate on, and trying to do more adds up to doing less.

CERTIFIED INSTRUCTORS IN THE PAULA METHOD

NAME	ADDRESS	TEL. NO.
Garbourg Paula	Hadera	
Avriel-Amzallag Michal	Moshav Carmel	02-961770
Achituv Tamar	Hatayassim St 17, Jerusalem	02-666339
Efrat Varda	Yisrael Zarhi St 56/7, Jerusalem	02-870076
Bernard Pat	Israel Ben-Zeev St 12 Ramot Gimmel	
	Jerusalem	02-865266
Dr. Mandelbrod Yitzhak	Etzel St 15/8 Jerusalem	02-815236 (w)02-815633
Zuckerman Aliza	Jerusalem	02-416457
Kruk Miriam	Kibbutz Netiv Halamed-Hey 99855	02-900377
	Rehovot	(w)08-450570
Karni Tova	Nataf, Mevaseret Jerusalem	02-340065
	& Jerusalem	02-340065
Takomi Erella	Herzel Blv 112, Jerusalem	02-439244
Ben-Ari Nurit	Kibbutz Yotvata 88820	07-357531
Barkan Dalit	Kibbutz Neot-Semadar	07-358111
Kaner Irit	Beersheba	07-234626
Ragolsky Kirat Smadar	Moshav Hazeva 86815	07-581395
Goldhammer Aya	Moshav Shilat 73188	08-261364
Levy Osnat	Hadror St 4 Yavne	08-421686
Maayany Meira	Moshav Kfar Bilu 76965	08-413386
Roth Edit	Gefen St 23, Mazkeret-Batya	08-349605
Simcha Uri	Kibbutz Netzer Sireni 70395	08-278210
Schneider Naomy	Moshav Shilat 73188	08-261933
Teiman Shlomit	Moshav Shilat 73188	08-261076
Avital Yudith	Derech Ben-Gurion St 259 Ramat-Gan	03-5718821
Agmon Yael	Melchet St 24, Tel-Aviv	03-5604260
Etinger Yoram	Yatkovsky St 6 Kfar Ganim Petah-Tikva	03-9218804
Asodi Yuval	Rashi St 62, Tel-Aviv	03-291197
Erez Meirav	Pinsker St 37, Tel-Aviv	(w)03-5284408
		03-6819429 – Jaffa
Bahat Avi	Beit Lehem St 6, Tel-Aviv	03-5254384
Ben-Tolila Shabbat	Pinsker 37, Tel-Aviv	(w)03-5284408
Corinne		03-6821847 – Jaffa
Harpaz Reuma	Berliner St 8, Ramat Aviv Tel-Aviv	03-6419597
Chavatselet Nadav	Michal St 17, Tel-Aviv	03-5466418
Yom-Tov Shlomit	Yiftah St 16, Ramat Hasharon	03-5402005
Yakor Michal	Hachashmonaim St 31, Tel-Aviv	03-5281197
Lewinsohn Marganit	Balfour St 45, Tel-Aviv	03-5602637
Magnat Yoela	6 Ben-Zion Blv, Tel-Aviv	03-299310
Mager-Kahana Iris	Refidim St 24/8, Maoz Aviv Tel-Aviv	03-6471368